Consciousness and Its Implications

Professor Daniel N. Robinson

THE TEACHING COMPANY ®

PUBLISHED BY:

THE TEACHING COMPANY
4840 Westfields Boulevard, Suite 500
Chantilly, Virginia 20151-2299
1-800-TEACH-12
Fax—703-378-3819
www.teach12.com

ISBN 1-59803-300-X

Daniel N. Robinson, Ph.D.

Philosophy Faculty, Oxford University
Distinguished Professor, Emeritus, Georgetown University

Daniel N. Robinson is a member of the Philosophy faculty at Oxford University, where he has lectured annually since 1991. He is also Distinguished Professor, Emeritus at Georgetown University, on whose faculty he served for 30 years. He was formerly Adjunct Professor of Psychology at Columbia University.

Professor Robinson earned his Ph.D. in neuropsychology from City University of New York. Prior to taking his position at Georgetown, he held positions at Amherst College, Princeton University, and Columbia University.

Professor Robinson is past president of two divisions of the American Psychological Association: The Division of History of Psychology and the Division of Theoretical and Philosophical Psychology.

Professor Robinson's publications cover an unusually wide range of disciplines, including law, philosophy of mind, brain sciences, psychology, moral philosophy, American history, and ancient history. He is former editor of the *Journal of Theoretical and Philosophical Psychology*. He is also the author or editor of more than 40 books, including *Praise and Blame: Moral Realism and Its Application*, *Wild Beasts & Idle Humours: The Insanity Defense from Antiquity to the Present*, *An Intellectual History of Psychology*, *The Mind: An Oxford Reader*, and *Aristotle's Psychology*.

In 2001, Professor Robinson received the Lifetime Achievement Award from the Division of History of Psychology of the American Psychological Association and the Distinguished Contribution Award from the Division of Theoretical and Philosophical Psychology of the American Psychological Association.

Table of Contents
Consciousness and Its Implications

Consciousness and Its Implications

Scope:

The subject of consciousness is among the most vexing in both philosophy and science, and no less tractable in psychology, where the conceptual problems are often neglected. As a "state," consciousness seems resistant to translation into physical terms and measurements, though its dependence on a healthy nervous system appears to be as close to a "cause-effect" relationship as any in the natural sciences.

The aim and scope of these 12 lectures must be modest, for the subject is as vast as that of human and animal awareness. What I hope to convey may be distilled into four main points: First, that consciousness and mental life are *sui generis*; they are not "like" anything else. They are not like anything that is material or physical and seem to require for their fuller understanding a science not yet available, if ever available. Second, what distinguishes consciousness (and the term presupposes consciousness *of* something) from all else is its *phenomenology*—there is something it is like to be "conscious" that is different from all other facts of nature. Third, conscious awareness is a power possessed by the normal percipient, including non-human percipients. This power is such that much that impinges on the sense organs is filtered out and sometimes only the weakest but the most "meaningful" of occurrences gains entrance. Fourth, such powers vary over the course of a lifetime, are subject to disease and defect, and thus, lead to questions of profound ethical consequence.

Here, then, is a topic in which science, philosophy, medicine, and ethics are merged, the result being issues at once intriguing and unsettling.

Lecture One
Zombies

Scope:

In this course, we will attempt to unravel the nature of consciousness, its provenance, and its function. We begin with an examination of the concept of the zombie, which functions effectively as a physical entity *without* consciousness. If a system can solve problems and process information without consciousness, of what value is consciousness? The question of ethics is raised if we consider that entities without consciousness cannot be judged for their actions. Could such an entity strive for moral improvement? The subject of consciousness is vast and varied and, as a philosophical problem, far from an easy solution.

Outline

I.   Our core questions in this course on consciousness are: What is it? How does it come about? What is it for?

    A. Popular speech is rife with references to consciousness. We talk about being "half conscious" or "unconscious" of something; the act of "daydreaming" reflects by contrast on a vividly conscious life; the patient in the emergency room is suffering a "loss of consciousness."

    B. Zombies, the "walking dead," accomplish what they do without consciousness.

        1. Philosophical zombies are different from the Hollywood version.

        2. They are created to test certain notions we have about the essence of mental life and the properties that life must have to qualify as "consciously" lived.

    C. Some years ago, Güven Güzeldere summarized various ways of configuring such entities and then understanding their nature.

        1. One might make a device that is indistinguishable from conscious human beings in the way it behaves, though its internal machinery would be nothing like our own (a *behavioral* zombie).

2. A better "fit" than the behavioral zombie is the *functional* zombie, which does and says what we do and say; its underlying systems function as ours do but do not include anything by way of consciousness, let alone self-consciousness.

3. The third kind of zombie, the *identical* zombie, has an anatomy fully identical with that of a human.

D. These three types of zombie capture the various ways philosophers have attempted to dissolve the seeming mystery of consciousness.

1. One solution to the problem of consciousness is behavioristic: X is properly regarded as "conscious" to the extent that its behavior is relevantly like that of anything that is regarded as being conscious.

2. Other philosophers might use more stringent criteria: Not only must there be behavioral similarities of the right sort, but these must come about in the right sort of way.

3. The behavior must express underlying physiological processes of just the sort that underlie our own actions and speech.

4. To the extent that the device functions the way we do, we are permitted to regard it as conscious in the relevant sense.

5. But this entity nonetheless has no consciousness as we understand that state; physical foundations are unable to account for the consciousness itself.

E. If not physical properties, what other properties are there? Consider a system entirely physical but nonetheless conscious. How does a system entirely and solely physical come to have this defining mental property?

F. Some philosophers reject the very idea of zombies in any terms that would settle issues in philosophy of mind.

1. Nigel Thomas, in his essay entitled "Zombie Killer," argued that the very foundational premise on which zombie examples are constructed is defective.

2. If we accept what is now widely endorsed by scientists and philosophers—that our own conscious experiences are nothing more than the result of our own brain and

bodily functions—then zombies are, indeed, problematical.

3. But if zombies are a conceptual possibility, then functionalism must be false.

G. In his essay "Does Consciousness Exist?" William James (1842–1910) argued that the function of "knowing," if not explained by "consciousness," must still be explained by *some* concept.

II. We recognize the difference between the mere registration of an event and our knowledge of it: our *knowing* it—which raises the question of the value of direct awareness.

A. Direct awareness is not a requirement for learning or memory. A computer's memory can take on whole megabytes of new information, while being unaware of the function it serves.

B. So what is consciousness good for? This begs the question of whether the best account of those defining features of human nature are to be understood within an essentially evolutionary context.

C. The more refined conceptions of evolutionary influences do not require that every property be useful.

1. Consciousness, it might be argued, is an epiphenomenon of evolution—like an architectural spandrel, it is not functional.

2. The fully adapted being is akin to the zombie, but, owing to the formation of that being, consciousness appears as a byproduct.

3. Thus, consciousness may be regarded as a product of evolution, but with no embarrassment to the theory of evolution, just in case consciousness has no real function.

D. To be a zombie may be like sleepwalking.

1. To be unaware implies having no conception of consciousness and self-consciousness in others.

2. What form of interaction might be possible among such entities? Could there be crime and punishment, moral improvement, an aesthetic dimension to life, and so on?

3. None of us would claim to be willing to live this sort of life because it is not as rich a life as ours.

E. What of such "dissociative" disorders as "multiple personalities" that might have someone conscious of being someone else, or of stages of infancy at which there is consciousness but no basis for its personalization, or sleep, or dream-states, or of *autoscopy* and near-death experiences?

III. The word *consciousness* did not take on its current meaning in English until late in the 17th century. John Locke's *An Essay Concerning Human Understanding* appeared in 1690 and made use of the term in a new way.

    A. Prior to Locke's interpretation of the term, Thomas Hobbes said that what is "conscious" is just what is understood in common.

    B. In Locke's work, consciousness takes on its private character, its contents found through introspection, by a mind able to examine its own content and that of no other.

    C. The word is problematical, and matters seem to become even more unsettled when we add a "self" to it.

Essential Reading:

Güzeldere, G., "Three Ways of Being a Zombie." Presented at the University of Arizona conference *Toward a Science of Consciousness*, April 8–13, 1996, Tucson, Arizona.

James, W., "Does Consciousness Exist?" *Journal of Philosophy, Psychology, and Scientific Methods* 1 (1904): 477–491.

Supplementary Reading:

Hobbes, T., *Leviathan* (1651), book 1, chapter 7, p. 31.

Locke, J., *An Essay Concerning Human Understanding,* book 2, chapter 1, section 19, p. 115.

Questions to Consider:

1. Since zombies seem to be able to do so much without consciousness, what might be the effect of consciousness should they possess it while doing just these things?

2. Can there really be zombies? Can there be a "caretaker" zombie who is nonetheless "unconscious"?

Lecture One—Transcript
Zombies

Here is a riddle: What is it that we are happy to lose every day, and not at all surprised to have returned the next day? And, of course, the answer is, consciousness. It's the most natural of our possessions and, as with the very air we breathe, it becomes an object of concern only when the supply of it seems to be threatened. However, as natural as it is, it stands as a very serious threat to any number of core convictions and assumptions in both philosophy and science. My aim in these twelve lectures is to make clear just what it is about consciousness that serves as such a challenge to these very convictions and core assumptions.

Additionally, I hope to make clear any number of peculiar features of consciousness, often overlooked as we enjoy its many gifts. Along the way, there will be opportunity to examine the related phenomenon of *self-consciousness*, and the vexing question of just how it is we know that someone else has consciousness, and the quite serious question of just why we ever needed consciousness in the first place.

So to express the aims of this series of lectures in the most general terms, I'd say that with respect to the matter of consciousness, our core questions will be these: What is it? How does it come about? And, what is it for? Well, time now to get into it.

Popular speech is rife with references to consciousness. Students often admit that during a lecture—perhaps not unlike this one—they were *half conscious,* their minds wandered near and far. Even without the benefit of Freudian psychology, persons often leave room for the possibility that something said or done was *unconscious* in its origins—fulfilling some unconscious motive. The act of *daydreaming* reflects by contrast on a vividly conscious life. Then, too, there's the patient in the emergency room, a source of great concern owing to the *loss of consciousness.* And in still other contexts, we tend to think of consciousness and sleep as opposites, though we are less sure of how to classify the dreams we seem to be living through.

Now, some of us are old enough to recall that "mission of the elect" back in the late 1960s to *raise consciousness.* Any number of demonstrations was to be *consciousness-raising;* though, at the time, the desired effect seems to have fallen some distance (if I may say so) from my own consciousness.

I will include some of these topics in later lectures, but I will not begin the series on any of these themes, interesting though they are. Instead, though it may seem odd at first, I prefer to begin with the topic of—ready?—zombies! Now, as it happens, these creatures or entities, as they are featured in grade-B Hollywood films, raise very interesting questions in philosophy of mind about the nature of consciousness itself.

In the Hollywood version, zombies come about through a form of voodoo. They are the walking dead, the undead but still not living, for they are lacking souls. Nonetheless, these soulless creatures do many of the things the rest of us do. They carry packages. They find their way around. Some might save cats caught in trees or carry children out of burning buildings. So if it's the Hollywood version, we have reason to believe that what zombies accomplish is accomplished without consciousness.

I believe the old 1968 thriller, the *Night of the Living Dead*, still enjoys something of a cult following. Using the Internet and Google, I discovered that the cast of relative unknowns included Marilyn Eastman, who played "Helen Cooper," the bug-eating zombie. I like this next one particularly—Charles Craig was the newscaster zombie. Two members of the posse were zombies, as was the cemetery caretaker. Note, then, the diverse employment possibilities that Hollywood made available to these soulless beings, and this surely gives pause, long enough for the appearance of, yes, the philosophers' zombies.

Now, philosophical zombies are different from the Hollywood version. They are created to test certain notions we have about the essence of mental life and the properties that such a life must have to qualify as *consciously* lived. We might ask whether an entity that saves a cat caught in a tree, or a child in a burning building, might be credited with, in some sense, a mental achievement, though perhaps not a *conscious* achievement.

More prosaically, we might ask whether an adding machine yielding correct sums is satisfying the criteria by which we designate acts as calculating or computational. After all, these are among the actions characteristic of mental life and, to that extent, we might say that devices performing such tasks are properly regarded as functioning in, let's say, a mental way, or at least intelligently. Nonetheless, we have no reason to believe that such devices do so with *consciousness*.

Now, rather more scrupulous than Hollywood filmmakers, philosophers are careful to distinguish between and among different kinds of zombies. Güven Güzeldere, some years ago, in a very lively essay titled "Three Ways of Being a Zombie," summarized various ways of configuring such entities and then understanding their nature in a philosophically rich way. In principle, one might make a device that is indistinguishable from conscious human beings in the way it behaves. It does and perhaps even says just the things we do and say, though its internal machinery or circuitry is nothing like our own and may even be based on principles utterly unlike those that govern human biology. Except for its gross behavior, we would not mistake this sort of thing for a neighbor and probably would not experience either empathy or sympathy, were we to see it taken apart in the machine shop.

Now, a better fit than the *behavioral zombie* is what we call the *functional zombie.* It not only does and says what we do and say, but its underlying systems function as ours do. We might think of such creations as a set of prosthetic limbs and sense organs designed to respond to the stimulations and conditions that give rise to our own behavior. They not only accomplish what we, by way of our own conscious life, might accomplish, but they appear to do so in the right sort of way. Now, contrast this with a restaurant robot that might be configured to heat the soup on the stove, only then to pour the contents into the washing machine. We would see in this a real gap in its functional equivalence to an actual cook.

The right sort of functional zombie is one that may well translate any number of biological functions into electrical input-output operations, each of its subsystems functioning as ours do, but without the addition of conscious awareness of anything. Where our receptors and neurons are activated by external physical stimulation, so, too, are the sensing devices of the functional zombie; but the achievements do not include or require anything by way of consciousness, let alone self-consciousness.

Now, most interesting of the three is the third kind of zombie, the *physically identical zombie,* whose structure matches human anatomy, cell for cell, organ for organ. It looks like one of us; its inner workings are just like ours; it behaves as we do. It's physically a veritable double. Were we to see one of these coming down the street, we would be more inclined to greet it than to run away from it. Were we to witness an operation on it, we certainly would hope that the loss of blood could be controlled and that a full recovery would soon follow.

Now, these three types of zombie capture the various ways philosophers have attempted to dissolve the seeming mystery of consciousness. One solution to the problem of consciousness is behavioristic: X is properly regarded as conscious to the extent that its behavior is relevantly like that of anything that is regarded itself as being conscious. Whatever it is about our neighbor's behavior that finds us imputing consciousness to her, we are permitted to use these same public data in imputing it to comparably behaving entities, including zombies and robots.

Other philosophers are inclined to impose a more stringent set of criteria. Not only must there be behavioral similarities of the right sort, but these must come about in the right sort of way. That is, the behavior must express underlying physiological processes of just that sort that underlie our own actions and our own speech. To the extent that the device functions the way we do, we are permitted to regard it as conscious in the relevant sense.

Now, suppose, however, that we have an actual, even a cellular copy of a human being, made up of biological bits and pieces, and functioning in just the manner of our own biological systems—that third zombie. Suppose further that it behaves as we tend to behave. We may have little reason now to withhold from it the property of consciousness; but then we face a dilemma: this entity, entirely like our own in its underlying systems—an entity that behaves as we do—nonetheless has no consciousness as we would understand that property or state. The conclusion we'd have to reach is that consciousness simply cannot be explained in terms of physical properties. If this other being shares all of our features at the level of very physical foundations, but is lacking in consciousness—which we have—then the physical foundations are unable to account for consciousness itself. So there's a dilemma.

But if not physical properties, what other properties are there? Must we invoke ghostlike properties? Consider now the other horn of the dilemma: a system entirely physical but nonetheless conscious. Now

9

the question is this: How does a system entirely and solely physical come to have this defining mental property?

It should not be surprising that some philosophers have seemingly avoided the dilemma by simply rejecting the very idea of zombies in any terms that would settle issues in philosophy of mind. In a carefully argued essay titled "Zombie Killer," Nigel Thomas argued that the very foundational premise on which the zombie examples are constructed is defective. The premise, as we've seen, is that a zombie behaves and functions as we do, but does so without consciousness. Zombies are stipulated as not having consciousness in that their representation of the external world—whether a world of roses, or music, or milk chocolate—is not accompanied by qualitative features of our conscious commerce with the things that bring about such experiences in us.

As Nigel Thomas says in his article, "A zombie can tell you that the rose before it is red, and it will wince and hastily withdraw its hand if it touches a hot stove; however, unlike us, it never experiences the quintessential redness, the 'raw feel' of red, or the awfulness and misery of burning pain."

If we accept what is now widely endorsed by scientists and philosophers—namely, that our own conscious experiences are nothing more than the result of our own brain and bodily functions—then zombies are, indeed, problematical. Again in Nigel Thomas's words:

> If zombies functionally equivalent to conscious [human beings] are a real conceptual possibility…then functionalism must be false, because we are admitting that two functionally indiscernible beings could be mentally different—one is conscious and the other is not… Likewise, if zombies *physically* equivalent to conscious [human beings] are a possibility, then physicalism must be false.

Functionalism, however, is a perspective on mind that lends itself to more than one meaning. The great William James caused a stir among philosophers and psychologists about a hundred years ago with his controversially titled essay, "Does Consciousness Exist?" In James's wonderfully affecting style, his no-nonsense candor, he put his case directly. I'm going to avail myself of a lengthy quotation from psychology's master craftsman. So here's a quote from William

James. I shouldn't even have to give the name; the quote itself would disclose the identity.

> I believe that "consciousness"…is on the point of disappearing altogether. It is the name of a nonentity, and has no right to a place among first principles. Those who still cling to it are clinging to a mere echo, the faint rumor left behind by the disappearing "soul" upon the air of philosophy… To deny plumply that "consciousness" exists seems so absurd on the face of it… I mean only to deny that the word stands for an entity, but to insist most emphatically that it does stand for a function. There is, I mean, no aboriginal stuff or quality of being, contrasted with that of which material objects are made, out of which our thoughts of them are made; but there is a function in experience which thoughts perform, and for the performance of which this quality of being is invoked. That function is knowing. "Consciousness" is supposed necessary to explain the fact that things not only are, but get reported, are known. Whoever blots out the notion of consciousness from his list of first principles must still provide in some way for that function's being carried on.

It is a very long quote, a very important one. James is no skeptic about thought. Whatever term we choose to employ, we recognize that the difference between the mere registration of an event and our knowledge of it—our knowing it—is a real distinction. There may be many things we know, of which we are not conscious, and this is especially obvious in the matter of knowing *how*. One who knows *how* to ride a bicycle is not conscious of all the sensory and motor adjustments and coordinations on which the performance depends. But although we can know *how* without conscious awareness, it would seem contradictory to claim that we could know *this* without conscious awareness.

Still, it remains an important question as to what this awareness adds to anything. If the system without consciousness can process information, and solve problems, and achieve significant ends, of what value is the addition of a direct awareness of all this? It's certainly not a requirement for further learning or for memory, at least if all we mean by learning and memory is the acquisition and retention of information. A computer's memory can take on whole megabytes of new information, and a file cabinet can store many pounds of the same. So it would seem that neither the computer nor the file cabinet is especially limited by being unaware of the functions it is serving. Well, in this manner of speaking, the computer achieves much without knowing anything, just as the file cabinet stores much without remembering anything. So just what is consciousness good for, after all? And if zombies were capable of hopefulness, why should any self-respecting zombie hope to be conscious?

Now, in one respect, just to ask the question, "What is consciousness good for?" is already to beg a very important and significant question, and that's the question of whether the best account of those defining features of human nature are to be understood—must be understood—within an essentially evolutionary context. If the only way we can explain such a property is by way of the selection pressures dictated by evolutionary theory; then, when we come to a property such as consciousness, the right question to ask *is,* "What is it good for?" What kind of advantage does it confer? What would be the disadvantage for creatures that could do all the things zombies do, but not possess consciousness into the bargain?

If it isn't too close to heresy these days, I would want to record my own skepticism—or at least my own reservations—about the proposition that any and every psychological property, every feature of mind and mental life, must finally be validated against the assumptions of evolutionary theory. There may be respects in which it's quite a nice thing to be conscious of one's own life and labor, though the fact of it may confer no evolutionary advantage whatever. In any case, we're certainly permitted to examine the nature of consciousness in a spirit of neutrality as regards theories about its value. It's of obvious value at the personal level to the one whose consciousness it is.

Of course, the more refined conceptions of evolutionary influences do not require that every property be patently useful or even useful at all. Some theorists have advanced the notion of *evolutionary spandrels*—borrowing here a term from architecture. Stephen Gould and Richard Lewontin developed this idea a number of years ago in a paper they titled, "The spandrels of San Marco and the Panglossian paradigm." (Don't you love it?)

The intersecting arches in the dome of St Mark's basilica in Venice result in handsome, repeating, triangular spaces; but these are, to use a technical term, *epiphenomena,* of the arrangement of the arches themselves. They are not functional in any structural, architectural sense. Well, consciousness, it might be argued, is an epiphenomenon of evolution, or so the argument would go. The fully adapted being is akin to the zombie; but, owing to the formation of that being, consciousness appears as a byproduct, as an epiphenomenon. Thus, consciousness may be regarded as a product of evolution, but with no embarrassment to the theory, just in case consciousness has no real function at all. On this account, the zombies are like the rest of us, but without spandrels—to which I would be inclined to say, with respect to a theory of that sort, let the buyer beware!

In some respects we already know, if not personally then by observations or reports about other persons, what it might be like to be a zombie; it might be something like sleepwalking. And we do know some things about somnambulism. It's more common in early childhood; it drops off quite sharply by the teen years. It has a fairly strong hereditary linkage but, in general, those suffering from the condition are otherwise in good health. On average, episodes of somnambulism last a matter of minutes, seldom more than 15 or 20 minutes. The form somnambulism takes varies from a placid touring of the bedroom or the house to fitful sprints as if attempting to resist capture. Zombie-like, the child's glassy eyes are open throughout, staring blankly, but seeing well enough to avoid objects and to reach seemingly intended destinations as the child quietly roams the house. Typically there's no recall of any of these somnambulistic episodes.

What is it that we would lose were life to be one long sleepwalk? What is it that's unavailable to an otherwise functional, problem-solving device, just in case it is lacking in awareness of itself and of its own performance? Some answers begin to dawn even as we raise the question. Thus unaware, the device must also have no conception of consciousness itself and of self-consciousness in others—no awareness that there are other minds. Now, what form of interaction might be possible among such entities? Could there be crime and punishment? Could there be moral improvement? Could there be an aesthetic dimension to life, not to mention a striving toward what is rather ambiguously referred to as a state of transcendence?

The somnambulist doesn't know what it's like to be a somnambulist, precisely because somnambulism strips one of those epistemic resources that let us know what it's like to be a certain kind of being.

Somnambulists can do things, but they can't know things. Except in an attempt to be an interesting disputant, none of us would claim to be as willing to live this sort of life as the one we are living by way of consciousness; not because the other life isn't worth living, but because it's not as rich a life.

Now, in our faithfulness to the received scientific authority of our own time, we wisely consult the brain sciences, evolutionary biology, and evolutionary psychology to benefit from a teaching that might deepen our understanding of consciousness as some sort of depersonalized property. All this, as if we wished to know more about how the heart actually moves blood around, or how the eardrum is protected when loud sounds are delivered. We are nonetheless confident that, unlike eardrums and cardiac physiology, our consciousness is our own, privately known uniquely, solely by the one whose conscious life it is; moreover, that its personally known contents can only be described for the benefit of others, but not directly known by them.

What then of so-called multiple personalities? Or of such dissociative disorders that might have someone conscious of being someone else? Or of states of fugue and delusion? Or of stages of infancy at which there is consciousness but no basis yet for its personalization? Or of that quarter or third of life when sleep renders each of us unconscious? Or of dream-states in which we enter a paradoxical state of strikingly heightened consciousness, only to awaken to the fact that we had been sleeping all along? Or of that Freudian landscape, in which much that is vividly apparent is but a camouflage and a deception?

What are we to make of research on autoscopy, where persons somehow see themselves from a place distant from their actual bodies? And near-death experiences in which conscious awareness seems to survive the termination of just those biological processes on which mental life is presumed to depend? It's certainly doubtful that all this and more will be credibly subsumed under the heading, "spandrel."

In light of all this, it's somewhat surprising that the very word *consciousness* did not take on its current meaning in English until quite late in the 17th century. John Locke's *Essay Concerning the Human Understanding* appeared in 1690 and made use of the term *consciousness* in a rather new way. The roots of the word, after all, are the Latin *cum* and *scio*—to know in the sense of what is shared within a community.

Earlier, Hobbes would say that what is conscious is just what is understood in common. He put it this way, somewhat quaintly, "Where two, or more men, know of one and the same fact, they are said to be Conscious of it one to another."

In Locke's work, consciousness takes on its private character, its contents found only through introspection, by a mind able to examine its own contents, and that of no other mind. How different is Locke's sense from Hobbes's. Locke says, "is the perception of what passes in a man's own mind. Can another man perceive that I am conscious of any thing, when I perceive it not myself? No man's knowledge here can go beyond his experience."

The word would wait for its Chinese equivalent until the 19th century; and this, presumably, is not because the Chinese lacked introspective powers of mind until the 19th century, let alone a language insufficiently rich to convey whatever is conveyed by the English word. Surely it's not the case that no one had engaged in introspection until Locke wrote his essay and used *consciousness* in a special philosophical sense. The word is problematical enough, and matters seem to become ever more unsettled when we add to it a *self* in order to come to grips—as I will in the next lecture—with *self-consciousness*.

We see, then, that the topic in these lectures has had a seemingly sudden birth, followed by a philosophically meandering journey, only to face in our own time challenges as to its reality, let alone its importance. Clearly, we have our work cut out for us.

Lecture Two
Self-Consciousness

Scope:

In this lecture, we consider the proposition that conscious life is grounded in the real essence of mind and, as such, is somehow insulated from the changes that might otherwise be brought about by mere "matter in motion." If the constituents of our own bodies continuously change, can we still retain an identifiable "self"? We again turn to the British empiricist John Locke (1632–1704) for his contribution to the issue.

Outline

I. What is the relationship between consciousness and knowledge?

   A. It is possible to imagine a zombie called George that responds to his name.

      1. What is unimaginable is his *knowing himself* to be George, because, presumably, a zombie does not "know" anything. To know something is to be conscious of it and zombies are not conscious.

      2. Consequently, they are not self-conscious.

   B. The claim "I am conscious of a rabbit in the garden" is different from the claim "I know there is a rabbit in the garden."

   C. There is a difference between being *conscious of* and being *conscious*.

      1. The former is always subject to error.

      2. Being conscious or aware is to be the possible subject of an experience, i.e., the *self*.

      3. In the older phenomenological literature, there is the common assumption that consciousness invariably includes a "self."

      4. For there to be knowledge, motives, desires, and beliefs, there must be consciousness, but these features of mental life are often in operation without the actor reflecting on all of them.

II. With *reflective* consciousness, the focus is on *self* as the subject or source, but who or what is "self"?

    A. We could argue that an old ship, *Old Faithful*, that has been extensively rebuilt, is no longer *Old Faithful*. Since none of the constituents of our bodies remains constant over time, it might be argued that there is no *self* as such, for everything about us physically changes from moment to moment.

    B. Against all this is a venerable philosophical conception of entities that retain their identity over time and independently of physical changes.

        1. On this understanding, a thing is what it is essentially, even if a number of so-called accidental changes are imposed on it.

        2. Intellectuals of the 17th century, especially Newton and Galileo, held that the last word on what really matters is to be provided by science.

        3. Thomas Hobbes (1588–1679) in his *De Corpore* of 1642 held that two distinguishable entities cannot be the same and that there was continuity of the person throughout the seasons of bodily change, given one condition.

    C. Hobbes set the stage for John Locke's analysis of the issue.

        1. In his *Essay Concerning Human Understanding*, Locke develops the distinction between "real" and "nominal" essences.

        2. What we come to regard as the "essence" of something arises from our own tendency to classify it in a manner that is convenient by our own lights.

        3. What will give Locke or anyone else that continuing identity that might have been incorrectly regarded as one's "real essence" is no more than that on which the various habits and dispositions of the mind settle.

        4. It is the manner in which human intelligence perceives and uses entities that determines their "nominal essence."

        5. Locke gave the problem of personal identity its modern formulation.

        6. Faithful to Newtonian science, Locke regarded the real essence of a thing to be beyond the power of sense, a congeries of sub-microscopic particles held together by gravitational forces but perceived in ways that generate such *nominal* characterizations as "Fellow of the Royal Society" or "a rational animal."

7. These characterizations arise from conventional discourse, the contingencies of culture and context, the nuances of perception, memory, and mental life.

8. Locke accepts that there is a real essence, but he rejects the claim that this is given to us in our observations of a thing.

D. Locke reduces personal identity itself to the merely contingent contents of consciousness: It is hostage to the limitations of memory and the vagaries of experience.

1. Locke's famous example of the prince and cobbler, the contents of whose respective consciousness were switched, tells us that each man will be "the same man" but not "the same person."

2. The "real essence" of neither is disclosed by such nominal features as a princely bearing or special skill in turning leather.

E. How does this all play out in the matter of self-consciousness and that vexing *self* of self-consciousness?

1. Older philosophical schools tend to identify self with soul, namely, with an enduring feature of the individual, immune to changes that otherwise alter the conditions of the body.

2. On this understanding, behind all the changes that might take place in the life of John Smith, there is an essential John Smith that remains unchanged throughout the seasons of life.

3. If Locke's metaphysical mission is one of "Newtonianizing" the mind, then the first step must be the elimination of such a worrisome, nonphysical item as the "essential" self and the seemingly dual nature of reality—partly physical and partly something else.

III. Locke is considered one of the fathers of British empiricism, which reduces all that is factually knowable to what is observable or subject to perception.

A. If a personal identity is analogous to *Old Faithful*, then to the extent to which various old planks of memory continue to be present in consciousness, the personal identity of the individual is preserved.

B. Locke's cobbler and prince will each be not merely the subject of experiences but will experience these as *his own* and, thus, as experiences that cannot be had in just this way by any other.

  1. The amnesiac is not lacking in self-consciousness, though he may have lost his Lockean "personal identity."

  2. Locke knew this; he granted that we know ourselves to be the subjects of our experience *intuitively* and not as a result of systematic observation.

IV. William James proposed that there were different senses of "self," including the "material" self, the "social" self, and the "spiritual" self.

  A. Considering the spiritual self at all is a reflective process.

  B. Locke thought our knowledge of God and of ourselves was "intuitive," whereas our knowledge of the necessary truths of geometry was "demonstrative" in that a formal argument is required to demonstrate the truth of the conclusions.

  C. Apart from these special cases, all of our factual knowledge comes, on Locke's account, from experience.

V. It is unclear that intuitive knowledge of one's self must be included among the necessary starting points in examining and defining consciousness.

  A. Zombies are mindless. If consciousness is not necessary to account for seemingly mental achievements, why would self-consciousness be requisite?

  B. Moreover, is it really the case that a person always knows *as a necessary truth and immediately* that the thoughts occupying consciousness are his own?

  C. If "normal" knowledge of consciousness depends on the brain's health and proper functioning, isn't it *contingent* rather than *necessary*?

Essential Reading:

James, W., *Principles of Psychology*, pp. 283–296.

Robinson, D. N., ed., *The Mind (Oxford Readers)*.

Supplementary Reading:

Bealer, G., "Self-consciousness," *Philosophical Review* 106: 69–117.

Questions to Consider:

1. In what sense might someone be conscious but not aware of himself or herself as the conscious entity?

2. If everything in the body (and brain) changes, minute-by-minute, how can our "self-consciousness" be explained in physical terms?

Lecture Two—Transcript
Self-Consciousness

I begin this second lecture with a line from that great classic, *The Night of the Living Dead*, which I discussed in the first lecture. This is what was said in that movie, and it's a good way to begin the second lecture: "If you kill the brain, you kill the ghoul." What is asserted here is that, without a functioning brain, the zombies would be finished. However, with their functioning brains, revived from death by radiation, they remain the living dead, which is to say, active, sensing, hungry beasts, able to find and, alas, devour human flesh, but in the manner of some gruesome robot.

If zombies are really like their portrayals, I can imagine one of them responding to the name, "George," and even running toward the Zombie Hotel when summoned by that name. What I cannot imagine is his knowing himself to be George, for a zombie presumably doesn't *know* anything. To know something is presumably to be conscious of it; and if the previous lecture reached a correct position on this matter, zombies aren't conscious. And, as they are not conscious, they certainly are not self-conscious.

Well, what about us? Are we conscious? And, except when sleeping, are we always conscious? And just what is that *self,* absent which one cannot be *self-conscious?* And just what is the relationship between consciousness and knowledge? These are questions I'll address in this second lecture.

Let me take the last question first, just to show that reasonable assumptions do not always pass philosophical muster. The claim, "I am conscious of a rabbit in the garden" is clearly different from the claim, "I know there is a rabbit in the garden," for one might well be conscious of what is actually a figment of the imagination. To know there is a rabbit in the garden requires, among other considerations, that indeed there *is* a rabbit in the garden. But to be conscious of a rabbit in the garden may be no more than to suffer from a kind of hallucination. Of course, one might also be utterly confused as to what one *knows* is in the garden.

But there's a difference between being mistaken about what is "out there" and being mistaken in assuming that there is anything out there. Put more directly, there's a difference between a mistake and a hallucination. There is also a difference between being *conscious of* and being *conscious*. The former is always subject to error; the latter, it seems, is quite different in this regard. Being conscious, or aware, is to be the possible subject of an experience, whether at any time there is in fact the specific experience of anything. One might think of this as a system being "on the air" though not yet tuned to any clear station or channel. The subject of possible experience is what in ordinary terms is often referred to as the *self*, as in *myself,* and it is to the concept of *self* that I now turn.

In the older phenomenological literature, there is the common assumption that consciousness invariably includes a self. As Edmund Husserl expressed it, "the self as such appears unfailingly with consciousness"—in Husserl's German phrase, *"Für-sich-selbst-erscheinens."* Here the German phrase captures the notion of consciousness as the simultaneous arrival or appearance of the self.

Sartre makes the same point when he takes self-consciousness to be the very mode of experience and not merely a property of it. Indeed, it is, he says, "the only mode of existence" for there to be a consciousness of anything at all.

Now in the more current idiom, the same notion is conveyed by the idea of what it is like to be the subject of experiences. Common though this way of phrasing the matter is, I'm wary of it, for it seems to require some sort of conceptual bridge to take us from, what it is like to have thoughts, desires, feelings, etc., across the bridge to ourselves as thinking, desiring, and feeling beings. I am going to try here to avoid the what-it-is-like-to-be locutions, even at the risk of philosophical naïveté. Instead, I will say straight away that every conscious moment is someone's, but that every conscious moment does not invariably focus on that fact.

If philosophical terms are useful in dealing with matters of this sort, I would say that there is a difference between what is called *unreflective* and *reflective* consciousness. It would be odd, after concluding the morning shower, for a person to maintain a disciplined conversation with herself, of the sort, "I am now looking in the mirror. I am now drying my right cheek. I am now looking for the talc." Rather, all sorts of semi-automatic initiatives are taken without any reflective self-consciousness at all on the part of the actor. For there to be knowledge, motives, desires, beliefs, there must be consciousness; but these features of mental life are often in operation without the actor reflecting on each, or all, of them; or perhaps even any of them.

Reflective consciousness is something else again. Here we recognize not only that conscious experience invariably includes self-consciousness, as what Sartre called "the mode of its very existence"; but the focus is on self as the subject or the source. But what or who is this self?

We might begin our inquiry by considering an old sailing vessel in serious need of repair. The wooden planks are rotten, the mast is wormy, and the sails are in shreds. Let's call the ship *Old Faithful*. Buying it at a cheap price, we have funds remaining to restore it to its pristine condition. We hire craftsmen and give them an ample enough budget to buy new wood and new sailing cloth. They proceed to remove each plank and replace it with new boards now sanded and covered with a high-quality marine shellac. In time we see *Old Faithful* as it might have appeared to its original crew. But is this *Old Faithful?* Should we not call it *Son of Old Faithful,* or *Old Faithful 2?*

Now suppose we take the old rotten planks and have the workmen assemble these to form another vessel, now made only of the original materials. In light of the difference in the composition of the two vessels, one would be hard pressed to decide which should be regarded as *Old Faithful.* One of the ships, fully repaired, shares none of the history of the original vessel. The other has all the original material but is scarcely seaworthy, scarcely a ship at all, for it cannot function as a ship. What if an observer aware of all this insists that neither vessel is *Old Faithful,* for *Old Faithful* disappeared when all of its constituents were removed. For something to be itself, it must have continuity over time.

Note, however, that none of the constituents of our own bodies remains constant over time; and, in light of that fact, it might be argued that there is no *self* as such, for everything about us physically changes from moment to moment. To the extent that our self just is all of these constituent parts working together in the proper way; and to the extent that each of these parts undergoes constant change, there simply cannot be an enduring self at all—or so one line of argument would have us believe.

Now against all this is a venerable philosophical conception of entities that do retain their identity over time, and independently of all physical changes. On this understanding, a thing is what it is, essentially, even if a number of so-called accidental changes happen to be imposed on it. Thus, even though Smith changes from infancy through childhood and into adulthood, there is some essential Smith whose identity remains constant.

Suppose Smith in childhood takes up the violin. We would say later that Smith is a musician; but we would mean something different from what we would mean when saying that Smith is a man. Smith could not be what he is, were he not a human being; but Smith would continue to be a human being had he never learned how to read music or play a musical instrument. In the language of Aristotle and his scholastic commentators, Smith is a man essentially; a musician, accidentally.

Let me move now to a later chapter in the history of thought, to those 17th century giants of scientific thought—especially Newton and Galileo—who persuaded the leading intellectuals of the age, and of following ages, that the last word on what really matters is to be provided by science. Increasingly, notions of essences and substances came under critical scrutiny.

The example of *Old Faithful* differs only slightly from an actual example discussed by Thomas Hobbes. In his example, it was the ancient ship of Theseus that was the subject of analysis. This is the ship that legend has, sailed by Theseus from the Greek mainland to the island of Crete, where King Minos had been appropriating Athenian youth for years, only to have them sacrificed to the beastly Minotaur, deep within the island's fabled Labyrinth. In freeing Athens from this horrid tyranny, Theseus became a great hero, his ship taken from port to port, year after year, in celebration of his great victory over the Minotaur. And, yes, in time the planks had to be replaced, as with our example of *Old Faithful*. Now, what does Thomas Hobbes have to say about this?

It's in his *De Corpore—Concerning the body—* published in 1642, that we find the chapter titled, "Of Identity and Diversity." It is in that chapter that he treats of the ship of Theseus. Regarding this ship, Hobbes says, in a manner both arcane and convinced:

> If…that ship of Theseus, concerning the difference whereof made by continual reparation in taking out the old planks and putting in the new, the Sophisters of Athens were wont to dispute, were, after all the planks were changed, the same

numerical ship it were at the beginning; and if some man had kept the old planks as they were taken out, and by afterwards putting them together in the same order, had again made a ship of them, this without doubt, had also been the same numerical ship…which it was in the beginning; and so there would have been two ships numerically the same, which is absurd.

Well, how shall we put it today? Two distinguishable entities cannot be the same. Hobbes must argue for a sense of identity that does not collapse into such absurdities. There is, of course, a sense in which the water in the river is the same as the water now forming the cloud. There is a sense in which it is different. There's a sense in which Socrates as a child is different from Socrates as a man. Regarding personal identity, we ask, what is the sense in which it has continuity amidst the corporeal fluxes of the hour and of the lifetime? Well, let's again consult Thomas Hobbes:

> …that man will always be the same, whose actions and thoughts all proceed from the same beginning of motion, namely that which was in his generation; and that will be the same river which flows from one and the same fountain, whether the same water, or other water, or something else than water, flow from thence; and that the same city, whose acts proceed continually from the same institution, whether the men be the same or no.

Here the ever-mechanistic thinker accepts the continuity of the person throughout the seasons of bodily change, so long as one condition is satisfied—and what is that?—"The same beginning of motion, namely that which was in his generation." Hobbes is rejecting here Aristotelian essences in favor of the identity of functional states. All in all, Hobbes's treatment would set the stage for John Locke's analysis of this same issue, and his own conclusions regarding the continuity of material *man* but the alteration of that man's *person*.

To see how Locke attempts to the render all this conformable to the science of his time, we begin with his anti-essentialism. In *An Essay Concerning Human Understanding,* Locke develops the distinction between what he called *real* and what he called *nominal* essences. The central thesis is developed in Book III, Chapter 6. Here Locke notes that any number of creatures of Locke's own general form, or of considerably different form, might have more or better faculties than Locke himself; but that such differences are not in any way, "essential to the one or the other, or to any individual whatever, till the mind refers it to some sort of species of things."

In other words, what we come to regard as the essence of something arises from our own tendency to classify or categorize it in a manner that is convenient or useful by our own lights. What will give Locke or anyone else that continuing identity that might have been incorrectly regarded as one's real essence is no more than that on which the various habits and dispositions of the mind happen to settle. What we come to regard as the essence of a thing, or of a person, is just a set of features to which we have reliable perceptual access and which are stable enough to permit classification.

Imagine the world and ourselves to be just what we are, with one exception: no one has ever eaten an apple or has ever been able to eat an apple. Rather, apples came to be used as—and were called—paperweights. We would by now agree that these round red objects that fall from trees are essentially paperweights. Here it is the manner in which human intelligence perceives and uses entities that will determine their "nominal essence"; that is, the essence they have as we name them to be the kinds of things we take them to be.

Following Hobbes, Locke gave the problem of personal identity its modern formulation. One of the aims of his *Essay* was precisely to challenge essentialism. Faithful to Newtonian science, Locke regarded the *real* essence of a thing to be beyond the powers of perception. The real essence is at the most fundamental, corpuscular structure of a thing, manifesting itself, if at all, only at that perceptible level on which variable, context-dependent nominal essences are fashioned. Locke's real essence is a congeries of submicroscopic particles held together by gravitational forces. But the perceptible Locke is that body of features generating such nominal characterizations as, "physician friend to the Earl of Shaftesbury," "Fellow of the Royal Society," "a rational animal," etc. These characterizations arise from conventional discourse; from the contingencies of culture and context; and from the nuances of perception, memory, and mental life.

It would be fair to say, in light of Locke's reference to the real essence of things, that he is what might be called an *ontological essentialist*— he does believe that there are essentially existing items—but agnostic at the level of epistemology. He accepts that there is a real essence, but he rejects the claim that this real essence is given to us in our observations of anything. Even if science were to attain perfected methods of measurement with which to identify the real essence of an item or entity, it would not match up with the manner in which we come to know and describe it. Consider quanta, for example.

Now, consistent with the distinction between real and nominal essences, Locke reduces personal identity to the merely contingent contents of consciousness, such that the notion of an essential self gives way to an identity that is hostage to the limitations of memory and the vagaries of experience.

There is an intimation of the real versus nominal distinction in Locke's famous example of the Prince and the Cobbler. The two of them, the Prince and the Cobbler, retire for the night. While each is sleeping, the contents of their respective consciousness are switched. Now, once the two awaken, Locke grants that each will be the same man, but not the same person. Each remains the same man—the reference here is to a physical body. But the person—as that person would disclose what he takes to be his essential self—is but a series of recollected experiences that constitute one as being a prince or a cobbler. The real essence of neither is disclosed by such nominal features as a princely bearing or special skill in turning leather. Locke is clear on this point. Personal identity, he says, consists:

> …not in the identity of substance, but, as I have said, in the identity of consciousness, wherein if Socrates and the present mayor of Queinborough agree, they are the same person: if the same Socrates waking and sleeping do not partake of the same consciousness, Socrates waking and sleeping is not the same person…

How does all this play out in the matter of self-consciousness and that vexing *self* of self-consciousness? Older philosophical schools tended to identify self with soul, which is to say, with an enduring feature of the individual, immune to changes that otherwise alter the conditions of the body. On this understanding, behind all the changes that might take place in the life of John Smith, there is an essential John Smith, his essential self—the spiritual center of his being—remains unchanged throughout the seasons of life.

If Locke's metaphysical mission is one of "Newtonianizing" the mind, then the first step must be the elimination of such worrisome nonphysical items as essential selves and the seemingly dual nature of reality, partly physical and partly—well, something else!

Locke is considered one of the fathers of British empiricism. The word itself is based on the ancient Greek for *observation* and *observer: empireia* and *empirikos*. In its various forms, empiricism reduces all that is factually knowable to what is observable, or to what is subject to perception. If there is a self, then, at least on this empirical account, it must be something subject to observation and perception, something answering to the data of experience. And if there is a continuing personal identity, then it too must be recognized at the level of perception.

For Locke, this had to be found within the contents of consciousness; or, more specifically, in the stores of memory. If we regard the personal identity of someone as analogous to *Old Faithful,* then we can say that, to the extent the various old planks of memory continue to be present in consciousness, the personal identity of the individual has been preserved.

But does any of this have anything to do with self-consciousness? I don't refer here to the shy person who is, as we say, too self-conscious, but to all of us in those times when we are awake, alert, and mindful—a good word, *mindful.*

Consider again Locke's example of the Prince and the Cobbler. After their conscious contents are transferred—the Prince's into the mind of the Cobbler, and vice versa—Locke tells us we now have *persons* switched, but not bodies. In today's hypothetical thought-experiments, the example would call for an exchange of brains. Locke tells us that the next day the two will awaken "the same man," but not "the same *person.*" To be the Prince is not to have a body of a specific type, but to have those spatio-temporally connected experiences that add up to what the Prince can call up into consciousness; and so, too, with the Cobbler.

However, even granting this much, it's still obvious that, on the next day, each will be aware, attentive, alert, and in a uniquely personal and mental contact with the surrounding world. Each will not merely be the subject of experiences, but will experience these as his own experiences—experiences that cannot be had in just this way by any other.

The person who is totally amnesic is not lacking in self-consciousness, though he may be said to have lost his Lockean personal identity. Now, Locke knew this much, which is why—for all this empiricistic commitment on his part—he granted that we know ourselves to be the subjects of our own experiences *intuitively* (his adverb), and surely not as a result of systematic observation.

William James faced the complexity of this issue head on and labored valiantly to keep both feet on the ground. In Chapter 10 of his *Principles of Psychology* he devotes an entire section to an analysis of the different senses of the self, including the material self, the social self, and, at last, the spiritual self. And of this he writes,

> I mean a man's inner or subjective being, his psychic faculties or dispositions. … These…are the most enduring and intimate part of the self, that which we most verily seem to be. … This spiritual self may be considered in various ways. We may divide it into faculties…isolating them one from another. … This is an *abstract* way of dealing with consciousness…or we may insist on a concrete view, and then the spiritual self in us will be either the entire stream of our personal consciousness, or the present "segment" or "section" of that stream, according as we take a broader or a narrower view. … But whether we take it abstractly or concretely, our considering the spiritual self at all is a reflective process, is the result of our abandoning the outward-looking point of view, and of our having become able to think of subjectivity as such, *to think ourselves as thinkers*.

It's hardly necessary to point out that we do not surround our thoughts about things with moment-to-moment reminders that the thoughts are ours and, therefore, that we can be confident that we are self-conscious. Nor do we contemplate deeply before reaching the confident belief that up is not down and black is not white. So when Locke speaks of something known intuitively, he employs the traditional and the essentially medieval criteria: What is known intuitively is known to be true; it's known to be necessarily true, and it's known without deliberation.

Locke thought our knowledge of God and of ourselves was intuitive in this sense; whereas our knowledge of the necessary truths of geometry would be demonstrative, in that formal argument would be required to demonstrate the truth of conclusions in geometry.

Now apart from these special cases—the intuitive and the demonstrative—Locke argued that all of our factual knowledge, all the information with which the mind is furnished, comes, in his terms, from experience.

That we know ourselves intuitively is a proposition, however, not without its own difficulties. If, indeed, this is how we know ourselves, it still seems odd to use a verb that generally stands for the acquisition of knowledge that can be shared. But if self-knowledge is intuitive, meaning that it arises from sources entirely internal, how can we know that there is any other self, any other consciousness? How can we know that there are other minds?

Moreover, to know oneself, intuitively or otherwise, should leave room for the possibility of being mistaken. That up is not down and that a thing cannot simultaneously be and not be are examples of what might be regarded as the starting point of all knowledge; but it's less clear that an intuitive knowledge of one's self must be included among the necessary starting points.

Zombies, if their behavior is to be successful at all, conform to the Law of Contradiction, even as we grant that they have no intuitive comprehension of it, for they are mindless. If consciousness is not necessary to account for seemingly mental achievements, why would self-consciousness be requisite?

And is it really the case that in all circumstances a person knows as a necessary truth and immediately that the thoughts occupying consciousness are his own? Might there be instances of pathology such that knowledge of this sort is less than certain and, therefore, not regarded as a necessary truth?

And if this is possible in instances of pathology, might the normal case depend on the health and proper functioning of the brain? And if this is so, then is not the knowledge in question actually contingent, and not necessary?

Well, later lectures will leave room for a consideration of this. For now, however, let's leave the ship of Theseus and *Old Faithful*, as well as Locke's Prince and Cobbler, and begin to think of just how it is we're sure that there are minds other than our own.

Lecture Three
The "Problem" of Consciousness

Scope:

In this lecture, we look at the perplexing relationship between the immaterial and the physical. We ask what it is about consciousness that would concern a physicist, and we address the claim that "physics is complete." We discover what Aristotle had to say about "real being," substance, and causality and raise the question of how the physical world interacts with a mental world not reducible to anything physical.

Outline

I. The core problem in the specialty of philosophy of mind is the problem of consciousness. Yet in our day-to-day affairs, we have no "problem" with consciousness; we scarcely think about it.

   A. Today, consciousness is an issue that tests both philosophers and theoretical physicists.

   B. Yet 18th-century leaders of thought were persuaded that no problem was inaccessible to the methods and perspective of the new physics.

     1. Pierre-Simon Laplace (1749–1827) summed up the confidence of his age when he claimed that if we had complete knowledge of the position and velocity of every particle in the universe, the direct application of Newton's laws would allow us to predict perfectly every future event.

     2. Laplace recognized that such complete knowledge was beyond the reach of human powers, but his bottom line, shared by a number of scientists today, was that physics is complete, even if our comprehension of its completeness is forever imperfect.

   C. This idea is ancient. The Greek atomists Leucippus and his student Democritus believed all of reality is exhausted by invisibly small physical particles and the spaces between them.

II. What does it mean to say that physics is complete?

   A. First, it adopts the metaphysical position—physicalism—that the only and ultimate reality is physical.

   B. The term *metaphysics* originated with 1st- and 2nd-century A.D. commentators on works by Aristotle (384–322 B.C.). They referred to the treatise Aristotle wrote after his treatise on natural science as *"meta ta phusica"*— "after the treatise on nature."

   C. Aristotle's *"meta ta phusica"* is the pioneering work in metaphysics, and its influence is nothing less than current.

   1. Aristotle declared it an inquiry into what really is, combined with a critical examination of the grounds on which we may claim to know this or anything else.

   2. The desire to know is not satisfied merely through sensory experiences. We know about things when we understand what brings them about and how they are related to other things.

   D. In Book I, Aristotle distinguishes among the different senses of "causation."

   1. Taking the example of an ordinary object, a coffee cup, one "cause" of the coffee cup is the matter of which it is composed—its *material* cause.

   2. But the material is insufficient to explain the causality associated with the cup. There must also be a *formal* cause for the cup to have the right shape.

   3. To produce the right shape, the cup must have an *efficient* cause, which explains how the cup came to have the shape it has.

   4. How did the makers of the cup know how to produce the cup? They had a plan to work from—what Aristotle calls the *final* cause.

   E. Aristotle's *Metaphysics* focuses on the issue of *real being*, and on this question, the limits of sense-based knowledge become evident.

   F. Physicalism regards all really existing things to be substantially physical. This invokes the notion of "substance."

G. For Aristotle, the substance of a thing is "that which is peculiar to it, which does not belong to anything else."

    1. We can say that Mary has a pain, not that a pain has Mary.

    2. Mary is not a predicate qualifying some other subject.

H. If the phrase "physics is complete" means that any and every entity to which real predicates are applicable is itself a physical substance, and if all predication in reality includes only physical properties, then "the problem of consciousness" is just one more problem to be solved by physicists.

I. If, however, consciousness is just a "code word" for an entity whose substantial nature is self-reflecting mental life, itself not reducible to anything physical, then the "problem of consciousness" is beyond the reach of physical analysis and physics is *not* complete.

J. In his *Metaphysics*, Aristotle addresses this issue with his categorization of real entities.

    1. *Sensible* entities are those whose being is readily established through perception and can be explained by science.

    2. Another class of entities comes under the heading of "unmovable"—changeless over time and in their essence.

III. We might postulate that "consciousness" is just that immoveable "substance" within the framework of which all change and all spatio-temporal affairs unfold and gain their real existence.

A. George Berkeley (1685–1753), early in the 18th century, concluded that the real, material world required for its subsistence a representation in *mind*.

B. On Berkeley's account, what is anything if not a set of perceptible properties? What is anything if not a representation in some consciousness?

C. The question at this point is ontological: What has "real being"; what really exists?

D. If physics is complete, we are committed to a monistic ontology of monistic materialism.

E. The problem of consciousness is one of discovering the manner in which entirely physical things and combinations of things come to generate a physical state or condition that we call "consciousness."

F. If, with George Berkeley, we find the most telling arguments being those that deny the independent reality of matter and require of the seemingly material world the foundational realty that is *mind*, then we retain a monistic ontology, but in this case, we would call it *monistic idealism*, real existence now being in the form of *idea*.

G. The more commonsense position to which we tend is that of dualism: There really is a physical world independent of us and a mental world of consciousness and its contents.

    1. If we adopt the position of dualism, however, we come up against the problem of explaining what kind of "stuff" this mental stuff is.

    2. If, as our commonsense ontology requires, it is immaterial, then we have the daunting question of just how an immaterial "desire to raise my arm" leads to my arm being raised.

H. Somewhere in this mix of questions and answers there seem to be assumptions that have not had the benefit of serious challenge.

    1. As with the medieval "problem" of witches, we often try to solve a problem by ignoring the real problem and developing a sound solution to a very different problem.

    2. As we shall see in subsequent lectures, there are a number of candidate problems, many candidate solutions, and much candidate evidence in the search for an explanation of consciousness.

Essential Reading:

Block, N., O. Flanagan, and G. Güzeldere, eds., *The Nature of Consciousness: Philosophical Debates*.

Chalmers, D. J., *The Conscious Mind: In Search of a Fundamental Theory*.

Supplementary Reading:

Flanagan, O. J., *Consciousness Reconsidered*.

Robinson, D. N., ed., *The Mind: (Oxford Readers)*.

Sartre, J., *Being and Nothingness*, p. 20.

Questions to Consider:

1. Earlier ages of philosophy reveal no concern about consciousness being a "problem." What modern developments have made it problematical?

2. If consciousness really is a "problem," where should we look for a solution? And why "there," instead of somewhere else?

Lecture Three—Transcript
The "Problem" of Consciousness

In the previous lecture I noted that consciousness becomes a still more complex phenomenon when considered in the context of self-consciousness. Clearly, we have a problem.

Well, perhaps it's time to break the news of what, to many beyond the reach of the graduate seminar, may come as a surprise; namely, it is the considered judgment of today's leading philosophers that the core problem in that specialty called philosophy of mind, just *is* the problem of consciousness. Listen to the philosopher John Searle on this point: "The most important scientific discovery of the present era will come when someone—or some group—discovers the answer to the following question: How exactly do neurobiological processes in the brain cause consciousness?"

In his "Facing up to the problem of consciousness," David Chalmers says straightaway, "Consciousness poses the most baffling problem in the science of the mind. There is nothing that we know more intimately than conscious experience, but there is nothing that is harder to explain." I quickly add that this same problem plagues specialists in fields as wide-ranging as theoretical physics and computer science, and may include more than a few theologians and ethicists. So, what's the problem?

Let's begin by acknowledging that in our day-to-day affairs—however we might identify ourselves by way of jobs, or professions, or vocations—we generally have no problem with consciousness; we scarcely think about it. Arguably, it's the most taken-for-granted condition of life. Even after the nightly sleep, during which time we've lost consciousness, it would be the more philosophically or maybe neurotically inclined who would have, as the first thought on awakening, "Alas, my consciousness has been restored!"

It's so natural that even children—who may be utterly perplexed by the question of where they came from or why the sky is blue—generally require no explanation whatever for the daily cycles of wakefulness and sleep, conscious life, and lengthy time-outs. Sleep produces what we take to be a natural, even needed loss of consciousness; and grave trauma or disease will produce an unnatural loss of consciousness. But apart from these occasions, consciousness itself seems no more problematical than our breathing.

In one interesting respect, what is unusual about consciousness being a weighty problem in philosophy is that, except for technical work in logic and philosophy of science, the problems of philosophy generally arise from matters that really do form part of the daily concerns of the average person. When we say in the course of a conversation something along the lines of, "I may be wrong, but it seems to me...," we record our awareness of the warrants we have for being certain about some matters—for example, "I have a toothache"—as opposed to the confidence we're allowed to have in our mere conjectures—for example, "You seem to have a toothache."

To put the point in academic terms, we can say that daily life presents us with problems of an epistemological nature, and it's one of the recognized tasks of philosophy to analyze the grounds of our knowledge opinions, our knowledge claims—our beliefs.

Consider also the ethical issues that arise within the course of a single day: Have I been fair and considerate in my behavior toward others? Am I failing in my responsibilities out of laziness or selfishness? Should I have agreed with Jack when he argued for a position I really disagree with? Was it right to get out of an engagement by way of a headache that wasn't really that severe? Shouldn't we invite the Smiths before we accept another invitation from them? Do I praise my children beyond their actual merits?

Now, questions such as these are not burning questions, but they do call for our attention because they are drawn from recognizable moral categories that sometimes *do* raise burning questions— questions of life and death, questions in which one's self-regarding motives may be at significant cost to others. And, obviously, questions of this nature should engage and have engaged the energies of whole generations of philosophers in the fields of ethics, philosophy of law, and moral philosophy.

Consciousness is, as I say, different in this respect, for it is at once entirely unproblematical for the ordinary person, but a source of continuing vexation for philosophy, as well as for specialists and scholars in several other areas.

Let me not foreclose debate here. When we find an issue that tests the powers of highly developed disciplines but causes no difficulty whatever at the level of daily life, we might be tempted to conclude that, here again, the plain folk just don't have the wits to see a real problem when there is one. However, there is another possibility; namely, that whatever it is that has resulted in the development of these disciplines, it is either misapplied to non-disciplinary contexts or is burdened by a problem largely of their own making.

Well, setting that aside for now, let's begin with theoretical physics, and ask just what it is about consciousness that a physicist should even consider, let alone worry about. I shall take this up more closely in a later lecture on consciousness and physics, but here let me briefly point to the dilemma caused by the facts of consciousness.

In the 18th century, at the height of the French Enlightenment, the scientific achievements of the previous century—the century of Newton and Galileo—the leaders of thought were persuaded that no problem was inaccessible to the methods and perspectives of the new physics. Pierre-Simon Laplace, born in 1749 and a productive mathematician and philosopher till his death in 1827, summed up the confidence of an entire age when he claimed that, if we had complete knowledge of the position and velocity of every particle in the universe, well, the direct application of Newton's laws would allow us to predict perfectly every future event. Here's how he stated it in his famous *Philosophical Essay on Probabilities:*

> We may regard the present state of the universe as the effect of its past and the cause of its future. An intellect which at a certain moment would know all forces that set nature in motion, and all positions of all items of which nature is composed, if this intellect were also vast enough to submit these data to analysis, it would embrace in a single formula the movements of the greatest bodies of the universe and those of the tiniest atoms; for such an intellect nothing would be uncertain and the future just like the past would be present before its eyes.

The intellect envisaged by Laplace—the entity that later would be dubbed Laplace's Demon—is not some very bright physicist at Cal Tech or MIT; nor is it something likely to be confused with our own human intellect. Think of it instead as a super-supercomputer, programmed with the physical dynamics of everything; that is to say, *everything.*

It is to Laplace's lasting credit that, recognizing such complete knowledge to be beyond the reach of human powers, he shifted his focus and contributed significantly to that very theory of probability that permits scientific prediction in the face of incomplete knowledge. But his bottom line, so to speak, shared by any number of leading scientists today, is captured in the maxim, "physics is complete," even if our comprehension of its completeness would be forever imperfect.

Well, this idea is ancient, of course. The Greek atomists, Leucippus and his student, Democritus, stood behind the proposition that all of reality is exhausted by invisibly small physical particles and the spaces between them. The word *atom,* after all, in its Greek etymology refers to that which cannot be cut any further—*a-tomos*—that which is ultimately small.

This view, taken quite seriously in the middle of the 5th century B.C., has waxed and waned in its influence on later ages; but it has always seemed to be redeemed by every stage in the progress of science. Epochs dominated by the confident belief that one thing or another could never be explained or accomplished were sooner or later superseded by ages of scientific discoveries that made the old impossibilities seem like child's play. As articles of faith go then, confidence in what science may ultimately explain is no mark of village credulity, but a plausible degree of confidence in that horse that has a habit of winning all the big races.

Well, what does it mean to say that physics is complete? To begin with, it is to adopt a metaphysical position, which can be classified as an *ism,* and in this case, the *ism* is physicalism. It is to adopt the position that the only and ultimate reality is physical; that everything is substantially physical in the traditional sense of substance, to which I will turn shortly.

But first some words about metaphysics, for it's one of those words that too often is permitted to mean nearly anything the speaker chooses. Its origin, however, is quite innocent. Commentators in the 1st and 2nd centuries A.D., in possession of works by Aristotle, assigned titles to Aristotle's treatises. One of these treatises referred to work just completed by Aristotle in his Lyceum, work on what we would translate as "natural science" or as " physics"—*phusis*—but physics in a very broad sense. Thus, the work that followed this one in time, the work next undertaken, was rather innocently classified by commentators as *meta ta phusica*, meaning no more than "after the treatise on nature."

The work itself, however, is among the least innocent in the entire library of philosophical thought. It is the pioneering work in metaphysics, and its influence can be described as nothing less than current. Aristotle declares its subject matter to be that of real being—an inquiry into what really is, combined with a critical examination of the grounds on which we may claim to know this or, for that matter, know anything.

It's worth pointing out that the very first book of the *Metaphysics* might well qualify as the first actual history of philosophy composed by a person of known identity; for in that, Aristotle reviews what others have said about the topics to be addressed. And though some he cites are clearly opponents of his own views, his coverage is fair and as thorough as would be expected in such summaries.

The very opening lines of the work are disarmingly direct. Aristotle says, "All men by nature desire to know." An example of this is "the delight we take in our senses." He insists that this very delight is not based solely on usefulness; rather, "our sensory commerce with the world and the knowledge thereby obtained will generate delight from the sheer activity itself," he says.

The desire to know, however, is not satisfied merely through sensory experiences. Rather, we regard ourselves as knowing about things and events when we understand what brings them about and how they are related to other things and events. It's in Book I that Aristotle refers to those very "causes" previously discussed in the treatise on natural science—the *phusis*—which carefully distinguishes among the different senses of causation. It will be useful to review this briefly.

Now, Aristotle's conception of causality continues to provide philosophy with grist for productive argument and analysis. Let's take as a way of illustrating his conception of an ordinary object, a coffee cup. We're called upon to answer the question, "What's the cause of this coffee cup?"

Now, clearly, for it to have been brought about at all, there must be some sort of matter capable of being worked on, capable of holding its shape, etc. Now, if what we mean by the cause of something must include whatever is necessary for a thing to exist at all, then surely, in one sense, the cause of the coffee cup is the matter of which it is composed. Thus does Aristotle include *material causes* among the causes of any object.

Now, noting the difference between a pile of bricks and a house, Aristotle goes on to point out that mere clumps of matter are insufficient to explain causality as associated with actual things. In our example, the raw material comes to be recognized as a coffee cup in virtue of having the proper shape, the right form. Now, if an object is a cup if and only if it has a form of a certain kind, then one of the necessary conditions that must be satisfied for it to be a cup just is a form—and this is the sense in which Aristotle refers to the *formal cause* of something.

In his treatise on physics, or natural science, Aristotle reminds us that—he puts it this way—"If the art of shipbuilding were in the wood, we would have ships by nature." What he makes clear is that one will never see an Athenian trireme, with its leather sails, its vertically arranged levels of oarsmen, its sharply honed planks, coming about simply as a result of natural forces working on matter over long periods of time. If you wish to have a trireme, it must be built; that is, skilled craftsmen must set to work on the material components and fashion them into the very form of a trireme. Each of the cuts in the wood, each blow of the hammers, each rope that stretches the sails, is a causal element in fashioning the end product. Each of these steps effects a desired alteration in the material; each enters into what Aristotle calls the *efficient cause* of the resulting ship.

But how does each worker know what to do? How do all of them, once their respective tasks are completed, produce the ship? Obviously, they're all working from plans. They are realizing a vision or blueprint originally formulated by the ship's designer. In the order of time, this blueprint is realized last; though in the order of conception, it is the first. It comes before the choice of materials and the choice of fashioning these into a given form. All of these subsidiary causal ingredients are to be understood as bringing about an object that serves a purpose, which allows a goal to be attained.

To understand what the final object is requires that we know what it's for—what its function is, what purpose or goal it serves. And this is what the ship's designer contemplated at the outset, and what the material, formal, and efficient causes ultimately led to. This ultimate plan and purpose is what Aristotle called the *final cause,* which, we might say, is the very reason behind the thing itself. Rejected in this account is the older Platonic teaching according to which the form of a thing is actually separate from the thing itself. As Aristotle says, "it would seem impossible that the substance and that of which it is a substance should exist apart."

We soon recognize, even before the conclusion of Book I, that this desire we have to know, and this delight we take in our senses, scarcely will touch that central issue to which Aristotle's *Metaphysics* is devoted: the issue of just what has *real* being. And on this question, the limits of sense-based knowledge become evident.

Let's now get back to the question of substance, which I said I'd return to. To say that, for example, physicalism regards all really existing things to be substantially physical is to invoke the notion of substance; and this invites us back into the pages of Aristotle's treatise. It is in Book VII, Part 1 of the *Metaphysics* that he explains the substance of a thing. He begins the section this way:

> There are several senses in which a thing may be said to "be"...for in one sense the "being" meant is "what a thing is" or a "this," and in another sense it means a quality or quantity or one of the other things that are predicated as these are. While "being" has all these senses, obviously that which "is" primarily is the "what," which indicates the substance of the thing.

He notes that such properties as "walking" and "being healthy" do exist as properties, but only in virtue of something primary. He says:

> It is that which walks or sits or is healthy that is an existent thing. [Now these are seen to be more real because there is something definite which underlies them; that is, the substance or individual]... Clearly then it is in virtue of this...that each of the others also is. Therefore that which is primarily [that is, not in a qualified sense but without qualification] must be substance.

Ah, Aristotle.

Well, later, in Part 13, he amplifies this main point, taking the substance of a thing to be, "that which is peculiar to it, which does not belong to anything else," and then goes on to say that, "substance means that which is not predicable of a subject."

We can say that Mary has a pain; we cannot say that a pain has Mary. Mary's substantial self on this account is unique. It can be qualified by any number of predicates: Mary is Irish; Mary is fond of Schubert; Mary is late for the opera. But Mary is not a predicate qualifying some other subject.

Now, if the phrase "physics is complete" means that any and every entity to which real predicates are applicable is itself a physical substance in this sense of *substance;* and if all predication in reality includes only physical properties; then the problem of consciousness is just one more problem to be solved—by whom?—by physicists.

If, however, consciousness is just a codeword for an entity whose substantial nature is self-reflecting mental life, itself not reducible to anything physical; then the "problem of consciousness" is beyond the reach of physical analysis; and alas—guess what?—physics is not complete—which is to say, that any complete account of reality cannot be rendered solely in physical terms.

Well, what does Aristotle say? In Part 6 of Book XII, he gets to the heart of the matter, reducing the possible kinds of real entities to three. One kind is in the category of the sensible, in that its *being* is readily established through perception. This might require all the aids to perception that technology can produce, including electron microscopes, the Hubble telescope, etc. Of these sensibles, some are permanent, such as the planets; whereas yet a second class includes things that come and go, such as plants and animals. All this, for Aristotle, comes under the heading of the *physical*, and is to be explained by physical science.

The third class of real things is different, and comes under the heading of what Aristotle refers to as the *unmovable*—changeless over time, and essentially what it is. Regarding this class he says:

> We must assert that it is necessary that there should be an eternal unmovable substance. For substances are the first of existing things, and if they are all destructible, all things are destructible. But it is impossible that movement should either have come into being or cease to be (for it must always have existed), or that time should. For there could not be a before and an after if time did not exist. Movement also is continuous, then, in the sense in which time is. … There must, then, be such a principle, whose very essence is

actuality. Further, then, these substances must be without matter; for they must be eternal, if anything is eternal. Therefore they must be actuality.

Ah, well, here this ancient philosopher teases us, from the distance of about 350 B.C., with an *ontology*—a study or science of real being—that includes as necessities actual, immaterial substances that constitute the starting point for all that will be in the realm of the changeable; all that moves in time.

Well, Aristotle aside, but with his suggestive ideas as a prompt, we might say that consciousness is just that immovable substance, so to speak, within the framework of which all change, all sensibles, all spatio-temporal affairs unfold and gain their real existence. Was this not the reasoning that led George Berkeley, early in the 18th century, to conclude that the real, material physical world requires for its subsistence a representation in mind? Was this not what Berkeley was getting at when insisting that *esse est percipi*—"to be is to be perceived"? After all, what can be meant by a blue sky, a ripe tomato, or the planet Jupiter, except as a constellation of experiences? On Berkeley's account, what is anything if not a set of perceptible properties? Now, tied to our current topic, we might ask, what is anything, if not a representation in *some* consciousness?

It might be a good time to pause to take stock of the basic kinds of substances on offer, so far as we try to get a firm grasp of consciousness and its problematic nature. As I indicated earlier, the question at this point is an ontological question—a question about just what has real being, just what we can say really exists. The Greek verb *to be* is *einai*. The Greek for *being* is *on*, the genitive of which is *ontis*. So, the subject of ontology just is that of *being*. If physics is complete, we are then committed to a monistic ontology; in this case, a monistic materialism. The problem of consciousness is just one of discovering the manner in which entirely physical things and combinations of physical things come to generate a physical state or condition, which we now call *consciousness.*

If, however, with George Berkeley, we find the most telling arguments to be those that deny the independent reality of matter, and require of the seemingly material world that foundational reality that is *mind;* then we retain a monistic ontology; but in this case we would call it monistic idealism, real existence now being in the form of idea.

The problem of consciousness now reverses itself. Now the task is one of accounting for the indubitable success, at the practical level, achieved on the assumption that there is indeed a mind-independent physical reality governed by laws, the adequacy of which has nothing to do with us or our ideas.

This all seems extreme, so we tend toward a more commonsense position, an ontology that we call dualism: there really is a physical world independent of us; there really is a mental world of consciousness and its contents. Now we can argue fruitfully about how or if these two distinct ontological domains are related; but that there are at least these two we regard as (I say at the commonsense level) obvious. Well, they are obvious until we press on with searching questions about just what kind of stuff this mental stuff is. If, as our common sense ontology requires, it is immaterial, then we have the daunting question of just how an immaterial desire to raise my arm, leads to my arm being raised. Equally daunting are questions of this sort: How can the physical discharges in the fibers of my optic nerve cause the immaterial conscious awareness of blue light?

Somewhere in this mix of questions and confident answers—for those who have adopted one or another solution to the problem of consciousness have in common a rather surprising confidence—there seems to be assumptions that have not had the benefit of serious challenge. It is not unusual for us to solve any number of problems by ignoring the real problem, and then developing a sound solution to what, in fact, is a very different problem. It's not unusual for us to assume that a solution must be of a given sort for, were it otherwise, we would face still other problems.

Mind you, when witches were being arrested for heresy, it was a matter of concern, to be sure, that the evidence of guilt was compelling. There was, we see, the problem of correctly identifying witches. On the assumption that such persons, owing to their pact with the Devil, would present clear symptoms—such as the inability to form tears—it became possible to develop standard procedures. The tests themselves were standardized, competently administered. There was an unnoticed problem here, however; namely, there are no witches.

Well, in succeeding lectures, I will trot out all sorts of candidate-solutions and candidate-problems—and, yes, candidate-evidence. I think we'll agree that some of it, even that which seems so leading-edge, is more akin to witches and their dry eye than to NASA and the Apollo program.

The task of science, here as elsewhere, is that of explanation. As I shall make clear in the next lecture, where consciousness is our subject, there seems to be something of a gap—an explanatory gap—which raises questions about how best to fill it in.

Lecture Four
The Explanatory Gap

Scope:

This lecture discusses the so-called *explanatory gap* that is inherent in the problem of consciousness. Philosophy of mind favors *foundational* explanations: The problem is seen as a gap between the dynamics of the nervous system and the nature of consciousness itself. Can causal relationships be established between neural events and conscious life? Some deny the existence of an explanatory gap at all. In the end, must we resign ourselves to the idea that this is just one of life's elusive facts?

Outline

I. If the major problem in philosophy of mind is the problem of consciousness, then it is so because of the so-called *explanatory gap*.

   A. Employment of the term *explanatory gap* suggests that consciousness resists location within the otherwise totally natural or physical domain and that were we to have the right sort of explanation, we would be able to move consciousness from a liminal location to the secure precincts of physical things.

   B. If the premise of an explanatory gap is accepted, then criteria must be developed to judge the quality of an explanation and its seeming validity.

   C. How do we explain the success of a trip to the Moon? One reasonable answer would be to claim that macro-level laws of physics must be correct because the mission successfully went to and returned from the Moon, based on the proposition that the laws of physics are correct.

II. The big gap in philosophy of mind has been seen as the gap between dynamics of the nervous system and the nature of consciousness itself.

   A. The majority of today's foremost philosophers would probably expect that gap to be filled by some sort of causal law.

B. For example, Jack is awakened by his alarm clock and says, "I'm going to be late for work." He seems to have moved from the state of unconsciousness to a state of consciousness. How can we determine what it was that moved him from one state to the next?

1. Common sense tells us that it was the alarm clock that awoke Jack.

2. But perhaps a more meaningful explanation might be given by establishing causal relationships between neural events and conscious life. Brain events unfailingly arouse one from sleep to consciousness, even without a loud sound.

3. Explanations based on brain function are more *foundational* than those based on the ordinary experiences of daily life. To know about brain function is to know what restores consciousness. To know about loud sounds is to know no such thing.

4. One basis on which to judge the quality of explanations is to consider as better the one that is applicable over a wider range of instances; that is, the better explanation is the more foundational one.

C. But it is not enough to say that Jack was restored to consciousness because of activity in his brain. We need to be more specific.

1. Yet even at a more molar level (neural units within the cranium), we still cannot find any intelligible means of connection between the mental state (i.e., consciousness) and some internal activity involving one set of structures but not some other set of structures.

2. Not every relationship is a causal relationship, nor does correlation imply causality.

III. There seems to be something of an explanatory gap between any number of paired relationships, where we sense that the first is somehow responsible for the second, but we cannot figure out how this responsibility is best understood.

A. Isaac Newton (1642–1727) accounted for the fall of objects toward the center of the Earth through gravity. But to cite gravity as the cause does not explain just how gravity has this effect.

B. David Hume (1711–1776), a leading figure in the Scottish Enlightenment of the 18th century, continues to exert an influence on the question of causation.

  1. Hume insisted that there is nothing in the external world that presents itself as a cause. We do not see, hear, or touch "causes."
  2. Hume claimed that all such causal attributions are based on experience, specifically, on what he called the "constant conjunction" of events.
  3. The explanatory gap existing between brain events and conscious experience is cut from the same cloth as the explanatory gap existing between the mass of objects and their behavior in free fall.

C. A contemporary philosopher, Michael Tye, argues that the notion of a "gap" is illusory. He reaches this conclusion by a complex analysis of how various concepts are formed and how they function at the level of our understanding of things.

  1. Take the visual experience of "red."
  2. According to physicalism, "red" = brain state "B."
  3. But, as Tye notes, this strikes us as unconvincing, for describing brain state "B" will be nothing like the experience of "red."
  4. Tye points to a basic confusion between the sense of a term and its reference.
  5. When we think of what it is that the left side of the equation is referring to, we just think in terms of phenomenal experience; we more or less "picture" red or redness, and in so doing, we absorb the left side of the equation into the conceptual realm of things "felt" or "experienced."
  6. Tye would have us accept the thesis that the actual references of our phenomenological expressions just constitute states of the brain; so-called *conscious* states simply *are* states of the brain under a different set of conceptual categories.

D. If the explanatory gap really exists, we still must ask whether it is a measure of where we have arrived in what is finally a work in progress or whether it promises to remain just one of those eternally elusive facts of mental life.

E. To assume that the explanatory gap is at once real and ineliminable in principle is to withdraw from this very framework at least one feature of reality, namely, our consciousness—which carries with it all the qualities that resist translation into ergs, volts, pints, and grams.

Essential Reading:

Levine, J., *Purple Haze: The Puzzle of Consciousness.*

McGinn, C., *The Mysterious Flame: Conscious Minds in a Material World.*

Supplementary Reading:

Tye, M., "Phenomenal Consciousness: The Explanatory Gap as a Cognitive Illusion," *Mind* 108: 705–725.

Questions to Consider:

1. What should any good explanation of a common occurrence include?

2. What are the grounds on which we regard an explanation as *explanatory?*

3. Where, within science and life, are there no "explanatory gaps"?

Lecture Four—Transcript

The Explanatory Gap

Philosophers have the amusing habit of classifying truly complex problems under misleadingly simple headings. If, as is widely believed, the major problem in philosophy of mind is the problem of consciousness, it is so, we learn, because of something rather innocently referred to as the explanatory gap. Hearing this, persons living outside the discourse, so to speak, might be inclined to think that there's some slight missing ingredient, which once provided, will settle this enduring problem. Why, all we have to do is fill in the gap!

I should begin this lecture, then, by searching a little more carefully to see what might be poured into such a gap in order to fill it, and what is on each side of it now that calls for a filling. The starting point is not the gap itself, except insofar as it puts some sort of space between, let's say, an X and a Y that shouldn't have this sort of separation. In the present instance, it's unclear as to whether the metaphor of a gap is really appropriate.

We are told that it is an explanatory gap, but this actually begs the question. As I hope to make clear, those who employ the phrase would hope to suggest by it that, unlike other common events, seems to resist location within the otherwise totally natural or physical ontological domain. That is, were we to have the right sort of explanation, we would be able to move consciousness from its currently limbo-like location to the secure precincts of physical things. But it surely cannot be only consciousness that is resistant to such a relocation. Virtually every expression of the aesthetic, moral, civic, and social dimensions of life seem strenuously resistant to translation into the language of physics or the natural sciences. Once real life enters into the equation, we seem to have gaps all over the place!

I shall not quibble, however. Let us agree, consistent with the spirit of the discourse, that there is an explanatory gap and that we should expect that the missing explanation, once found, will not only fill in the gap but will allow the terms on each side of it either to be collapsed into a single term or shown to be related to each other in some direct and unsurprising way.

To be clearer on what is sought here, let us test some explanations routinely offered to fill in a gap between events we think require explaining. Angela leaves the house and drives her car to a shop named Marty's Pizza. Angela returns to her apartment carrying a large square box. Twenty minutes later, Beverly arrives at Angela's, carrying a grocery bag. We are now asked for an explanation that will render these two sets of events somehow intelligibly related. Here are some candidate explanations:

First: Angela and Beverly had arranged earlier to share a pizza and to talk things over at Angela's apartment. Angela agreed to buy the pizza, and Beverly agreed to bring a beverage.

Second: Perhaps this is a better explanation. Angela and Beverly are tuned into each other's thoughts through a psychic network. Knowing that Angela has bought a pizza, Beverly also knows that Angela has forgotten to buy something to have with the pizza. She thereupon goes to the store, buys two bottles of a soft drink, and makes her way to Angela's apartment.

Third: Well, we might instead fill the gap this way: Angela came home with a pizza and Beverly simply arrived at the wrong address and knocked on the wrong door.

Now, how do we choose, from among candidate explanations, the one that seems just right to fill an explanatory gap? What criteria matter most as we set out to judge the quality of an explanation or its seeming validity, its aptness? Suppose we turn from a fairly mundane setting in which people decide to share a pizza to the astonishing setting in which astronauts are sent to the moon and brought back to earth. How do we explain the success of that sort of mission? I refer here not to an explanation of just why it was that vast resources were devoted to such a project; that, too, requires an explanation. I refer instead to how we explain the very success of the mission.

I think we'll agree that surely one explanation for the success of the mission is that the scientific laws on which the entire project was based are correct or true in that, if they weren't, the mission would have failed. So if someone were to say, "What makes you think the basic laws of physics at the macro-level are correct?" one reasonable answer would be this: "Because we've gone to the moon and have returned from there to earth, and we did all this based on the assumption that our laws of physics are correct."

In our mundane example, let's say that we know that Angela and Beverly are friends, that they meet on a regular basis, that they both like pizza, and this permits us to rule out explanations based on the assumption that Beverly arrived at the wrong address. And we may have still other and good reasons to reject the idea that they or anyone else is part of a psychic network.

Now, in the matter of consciousness, where is the big gap in philosophy of mind? Many believe it's the gap between the dynamics of the nervous system and the nature of consciousness itself. If we were to sample the opinions of today's major philosophers, I would guess that the majority would expect that gap to be filled by some sort of causal law. On such an account, if brain states of type X, Y, and Z take place, these somehow bring about, in the causal sense of bringing something about—lo and behold—consciousness.

But let's return to examples of the sort I previously cited. Jack is asleep as best we can tell, and then his alarm clock rings loudly. We see that Jack sits up in bed, his eyes wide open, and he says, "Oh dear, I'm going to be late for work." He seems to have moved from the state of unconsciousness to a state of consciousness, and what we're looking for is an explanation by which we can determine what it was that moved him from one of those states to the next. One explanation is that he was awakened by his alarm clock—no surprise there. Others might want to say that the sound of the alarm clock stimulated his auditory nerves, which sent a strong signal to areas of the brain, and that, through the activity of the brain, Jack was moved from an unconscious to a conscious state. His brain triggered the necessary processes.

At the level of common sense, it's quite clear that the alarm clock or any other loud sound would serve as a very good explanation of what awakens someone. This would have been a good explanation at times in human history when no one even knew there was a brain. Suppose the example was the caveman being awakened by the sound of a rock falling. Pressed to explain this event, others in the cave might be inclined to say that he was moved from the state of unconsciousness to a state of consciousness by the loud sound of a falling rock. We might suppose that this account was given before the language of the caveman included the word *brain*. What we have here are candidate explanations, one based on the presumed functions of the human nervous system and another based on the day-to-day experiences that allow ordinary people to form cause–effect explanations for events they've been able to experience frequently and make use of practically.

Granting that causal explanations at this level are entirely useful, we might press on to consider whether a fuller explanation—a more meaningful and even more useful explanation—might be given by establishing causal relationships between neural events and conscious life. Even more boldly, we might press on further in search of explanations based on specific brain processes judged to be truer and certainly more complete.

To defend this perspective, we might note the unfailing success of brain events in arousing one from sleep to consciousness. Brain events will do so unfailingly, even if there's no loud sound. Furthermore, it might be noted that, were there no such functional activity in the brain, nothing in the external world *could* bring about consciousness. To the extent that this is so, we would then be prepared to say that explanations based on brain function are far more foundational than those based on the ordinary experiences of daily life. We would go so far as to say that, with the knowledge of brain function, we can explain why the alarm clock has its effects; whereas no knowledge of alarm clocks as such, no matter how thorough, will provide us with an explanation of the effect they might have on consciousness. To know about brain function is to know what restores consciousness. To know about loud sounds is to know no such thing.

Well here, then, is one basis upon which to judge the quality of explanations: All other considerations being equal, the better of two explanations is the one that is applicable over a wider range of instances. Put a different way, the better explanation is the one that is more foundational. Explanation A is more foundational than Explanation B when Explanation A serves to account for the success of Explanation B; but not vice versa.

This is surely not enough, however. Terms such as *mechanisms, processes,* and *states* are really terms of art. I don't think those who speak of brain mechanisms really have in mind anything mechanical. Nor is it clear just what is meant by a state. After all, that word is based on the Latin *stasis,* which conveys the idea of something stationary, or in place, standing still—features never true of a functional brain.

And *brain* itself is quite a gross term for what in fact are billions and billions of interconnections among the neural units within the cranium. The units themselves are only units at one level; at the more foundational level, the so-called units are constituted of proteins, salts, water—these, in turn, being composed of various elements; and these, in turn, of atoms further reducible to subatomic particles. So to accept *brain function* as more foundational than, say, loud sounds in explaining the transition from sleep to wakefulness, we leave ourselves open to the question, "Well, why not say instead that the cause of Jack's restored consciousness was a collection of subatomic particles in his cranium?"

The interesting thing about subatomic particles is that they're really all alike. So we have to consider them in a very special arrangement if we're to get to the level of cells at all. But not just any cells will do. They must be cells in the brain, and in specific regions of the brain. So it would not be enough to say that Jack was restored to consciousness because of activity in his brain. We would have to say that he was restored to consciousness because of activity in a specific region of the brain.

This, in turn, establishes yet another explanatory gap. For we now have to account for the fact that not just any region of the brain is associated with the restoration of consciousness. It's really only this region, with this cluster of structures. Yet when we look at this cluster of structures, there isn't anything about them that seems any more related to the restoration of consciousness than any other cluster of structures within the same cranium. It seems that, in moving to the most foundational level, we've lost all explanatory power. Even in focusing our attention at a more molar level, we still can't find any intelligible mode of connection between the mental state about which we have no doubts—namely consciousness—and some internal activity involving one set of structures but not some other set of structures.

Might our difficulties be based on the possibility that we're searching for the wrong kind of explanation when we try to establish some *causal* relationship between activity in the brain and the mental state of consciousness? After all, not every relationship is a causal relationship. Jack and Jill are cousins, but they're not cousins because Jack caused Jill or Jill caused Jack to be a cousin. I would guess that one of the first lectures given in any introductory course in statistics includes the warning that correlation does not imply causality. There may be a very strong relationship between things and nonetheless not a causal relationship at all.

Well, this brings us face to face with a philosophical problem that's extremely difficult, quite apart from the issues of consciousness and mental life. I refer to the problem of causation itself. Thanks to Isaac Newton, we know that objects fall toward the center of the earth, and we have a term to account for what it is that seems to be pulling them there; namely, gravity. We even have precise equations establishing the relationship between the mass of an object and its free-fall dynamics.

In a manner of speaking, we can say that gravity is the cause of the behavior of falling objects. But this doesn't help very much if the question is just how gravity or the force of gravity has this effect. I mention this to make clear that this, too, seems to be another explanatory gap, and one obtaining between any number of paired relationships. The attraction between two bodies is proportional to their masses, but just why *this* is the relationship rather than some other, is not revealed by the law itself. Just what is it in the mass of an object that results in—which is to say, *causes*—gravitational effects? This is a question where the answers remain obscure.

One of the most influential philosophers was David Hume, a leading figure in the Scottish Enlightenment of the 18th century. His influence continues into our own time on any number of philosophical issues, especially that of causation. Hume is another in that line of British empiricists arguing that our knowledge of what we take to be reality is rooted firmly in experience.

In explaining how we arrive at the very notion of causation, Hume insisted if there were nothing in the external world that presented itself, we could have no sense of cause. That is to say, we do not see, or hear, or touch causes, as such—we don't see causes. So what, then, is the basis of our claim that one object or event is the cause of another? Hume's theory is that all such causal attributions are based on experience, and specifically, on what he referred to as the *constant conjunction* of events. Thus, when one event is reliably associated with another in our experience, we come to regard the former as the cause of the latter. This is simply the result of how the mind is constituted, how it operates. It's nothing but a habit of the mind to treat such constantly conjoined experiences as causal in nature.

Now, a small library of criticism has grown over the years in response to Hume's theory of causation, and this is not the lecture in which to explore the assets and liabilities of that theory. Surely those who regard the achievements in physics to be based on a grasp of how the cosmos really works will reject any notion of causality that takes it to be little more than a habit of the mind! One of the very influential contemporary critics of Hume's view is Wesley Salmon, whose book, *Causality and Explanation,* which came out in 1998, developed and defended a model of explanation called *ontic explanation.* Recall *ontology* as the term applied to the study of just what really exists. Salmon's philosophy of science is based on the claim that science provides accounts of real causal dependencies, for it discovers real—that is to say, *ontic*—causal processes and events. This is obviously opposed to Hume.

As I say, this is an important issue but cannot be pursued further here. Instead, we might allow ourselves to be just Humean enough to say that, if there is a highly reliable relationship between events taking place in the brain—particularly in cases of pathology—and resulting alterations in the conscious life; then based on the reliability of these relationships—and if only as a habit of the mind—we come to regard the brain events as causally responsible for the mental events, period. Our so-called habit, here, being no different from the manner in which it expresses itself in any setting in which we claim to know the causes of things, including physics.

Now, taking this position, we might then comfort ourselves by noting that the explanatory gap existing between brain events and conscious experience is cut from the same cloth—to mix the metaphors—as the explanatory gap existing between, say, the mass of objects and their behavior in free fall.

I say there is a comfort here. But at a metaphysical level we know enough to remain uneasy. The uneasiness arises from the recognition, however faint, that there's something special about the gap where consciousness is involved. A contemporary philosopher, Michael Tye, who has given sustained attention to the problem, offers a neat account of the staying power of the gap in the matter of consciousness. Let me convey some lines of his, published a few years back in the journal *Mind.* There he wrote:

> Once one learns that in solid things, the molecules are not free to move around as they are in liquids, one immediately grasps that solid things do not pour easily, that they tend to retain their shape and volume. Having been told the physical story, to ask: "Yes, but why are things with molecules that are fixed in place solid? Why shouldn't such things not be

solid?" is to show a conceptual confusion. One who responds in this way simply does not understand the ordinary notion of solidity. … In the case of phenomenal consciousness, however, the corresponding questions remain even for those who understand full well the relevant phenomenal terms and who know the underlying physical and functional story. One who has a complete understanding of the term "pain," for example, and who is fully apprised of the physical facts, as we now know them, can still coherently ask why so-and-so brain processes or functional states feel the way pains do or why these processes feel any way at all. In this case, it seems that as far as our understanding goes *something important is missing*. Herein lies the famous "explanatory gap" for consciousness.

Well, I take this lengthy passage from Michael Tye, not only because of the clarity with which he expresses the problem, but because he then rejects out of hand that there really is a problem! Note the title of the article from which this long passage was taken: "Phenomenal Consciousness: the Explanatory Gap as Cognitive Illusion."

Michael Tye regards the very notion of a gap to be illusory. He reaches this conclusion through a complex analysis of how various concepts are formed, and then how they function at the level of our understanding of things. His argument proceeds from his own example. Take the visual experience *red*. According to physicalism, *red* equals brain state *B*. But, as Michael Tye notes, this strikes us as unconvincing, for the very phenomenology of the experience, as Tye says, "isn't captured by the right-hand side" of the equation. None of the things I'd be prepared to say in describing brain state *B* will be anything like my experience of red.

But on this point, Michael Tye points to what he takes to be a basic confusion: a confusion between the sense of a term and its reference. When we think of what it is that the left side of the equation is referring to, we just think in terms of phenomenal experience—red. We more or less picture red or redness, and in so doing we absorb the left side of the equation into the conceptual realm of things felt or experienced. That is, again to use Tye's phrasing, "We bring it under a concept that has a distinctive functional role." Well, this naturally gives rise to a triggering of visual images of red items. But, says Tye, "If the identity is true, our brain actually goes into brain state *B*."

Note, then, that the sense we attach to the concept of seeing something red is different from the reference of the expression. Tye would have us accept the thesis that the actual reference of our phenomenological expressions just constitutes states of the brain. In this, he joins an entire school of contemporary philosophers who no longer seek the means by which brain states cause conscious states; rather, so-called conscious states simply *are* states of the brain under a different set of conceptual categories.

If I'm not mistaken, the first one to employ the phrase *explanatory gap* in the way that philosophers now wrestle with it was Joseph Levine, in a 1983 article titled, "Materialism and qualia: the explanatory gap." If there is this gap, we still must ask whether it is a measure of where we have arrived in what is, finally, a work in progress; or whether it promises to remain just one of those eternally elusive facts of life—in this case, facts of mental life.

To assume it is a roadblock of sorts faced by what, in the end, is the scientific community, is simply to repeat confidence in the completeness of physics; confidence that the right *ontology* is a monistic ontology and that, under that heading, nonphysical entities need not apply! If there are souls and angels, they fall within the pattern of real physical events and, thus, are to be found somewhere within the framework of real causal relationships. To assume, on the contrary, that the explanatory gap is at once real and unable to be eliminated in principle is to withdraw from this very framework at least one feature of reality; namely, our consciousness, which carries with it all the qualities that resist translation into ergs, volts, pints, and grams.

I should think the final holdouts for preserving the gap against the all-embracing inclusiveness of science would be the poets. In this connection, my thoughts turn to two luminaries of Victorian England, William Whewell (and anybody who wants to know how you can get a pronunciation "H-you-el" out of W-H-E-W-E-L-L must look into remote Celtic sources) and Alfred Lord Tennyson. Now what, you may ask, have these two in common? Well, to begin, Whewell was Tennyson's tutor at Cambridge, and at a time when Whewell was widely recognized as one of the finest philosophical and scientific minds in the realm. In fact, at the prodding of Coleridge, it was Whewell who actually coined the word *scientist*, even as he influenced the thought and work of such scientific geniuses as Michael Faraday and Charles Darwin.

Cambridge was ablaze in those years with young men of extraordinary talent and promise. A handful of the brightest formed the famous group known as the Apostles and included Tennyson and his very close friend and fellow poet, Arthur Hallam, who was soon engaged to Tennyson's sister. Expected to rise to the stratosphere of the British intelligentsia, Hallam died instead at the age of 22. Tennyson expressed his grief in that timeless work, *In Memoriam,* which took some 17 years to complete. In the final version, *In Memoriam* leaves behind all the nuts and bolts of Whewell's world, Whewell's science, the world of the confident scientist, and comes to grip again with the gap—here, the gap created by the death of a friend and of all the poetry thereby withheld from the world. Here are the lines we find in Section 120:

> I trust I have not wasted breath:
> I think we are not wholly brain,
> Magnetic mockeries; not in vain,
> Like Paul with beasts, I fought with Death;
>
> Not only cunning casts in clay;
> Let Science prove we are, and then
> What matter Science unto men,
> At least to me? I would not stay.
>
> Let him, the wiser man who spring
> Hereafter, up from childhood shape
> His action like the greater ape,
> But I was born to other things

We see, then, that there is this gap. It manifests itself in several ways. Perhaps most vividly, it presents itself when we set out to explain how it is that mental events cause us to act—the question that will occupy us in the next lecture. Mental causation: how is it possible?

Lecture Five
Mental Causation

Scope:

While causal relationships might be plausibly defended in attempts to close the explanatory gap, they pose problems. How can a mental activity cause a physical activity? A physicalistic solution is unsatisfactory because mental life is not reducible into physicalistic terms and concepts. It can be argued that matters of causation are principally matters of science, not philosophy. Moreover, much of daily life does not lend itself to causal explanations.

Outline

I. Causal relationships are serious contenders to close the explanatory gap in the relationship between mental and physical events, but they face serious problems.

   A. It is customary to expect in any causal relationship that the antecedent-consequent events (causes and effects) will be of a kindred type.

   1. Examples such as billiard balls colliding demonstrate action that takes place between two physical bodies.

   2. Can the same be said of mental causation? How can a decision I take to make a glass of iced tea make parts of my body move?

   3. At the commonsense level, and in the ordinary affairs of life, we take for granted that the plans and purposes shaped within our own mental life causally bring about actions capable of realizing those very plans and purposes.

   4. Considered philosophically, however, this state of affairs is highly perplexing. And considered scientifically, it seems virtually impossible.

   B. One solution to this problem is to adopt a form of physicalism and insist that decisions, judgments, plans, and purposes are simply code words for events in the brain, but this approach is flawed.

   1. If we were to recast all statements that we have made about our decisions, judgments, plans, and purposes in

physicalistic language, our statements would be unintelligible.

2. If we were to try to match up all of the characteristics of physical events with all of the characteristics of mental events, nothing would match.

C. Many philosophers have coupled a physicalist explanation with another explanation to satisfy the inherent problems of the physicalist approach.

1. Donald Davidson (1917–2003) defended the thesis that he labeled *anomalous monism*.

2. Davidson's monistic ontology proposed that there is only one kind of stuff in reality: physical stuff; yet mental life is not reducible or directly translatable into physicalistic terms and concepts.

3. The "anomaly" is that, on Davidson's account, mental events and processes *do* bring about physical events in just the sense of strict causation.

4. To do this, they must be physical but of such a nature as to preclude reduction to the terms of the physical sciences.

5. This is *anomalous*, for we are required to retain a dualistic vocabulary even as we acknowledge a monistic reality—hence, *anomalous monism*.

6. The most obvious criticism of this view is that it permits the very mental properties that make the causal model problematical.

7. If Davidson were willing to permit mental properties and, at the same time, regard them as irreducible to physical properties, this begs the question: How did these mental properties get caused by the physical properties of the brain?

8. Davidson resisted the very notion of properties and the conventional view that one thing causes another through some sort of causal mechanism that requires identification.

9. Instead, he took the position that where there is causation, one thing causes another by just causing it!

10. His skepticism regarding "properties" is echoed by other philosophers who have argued that "properties" are simply ensembles of causes. For example, to say that

water is a "universal solvent" is to say that it *causes* things to dissolve.

II. To answer the question **"What is a mental property?"** we need to identify mental entities.

   A. The most obvious mental entities are experiences and thoughts.

      1. It is not clear how we should convert the experience or perception of an object into a mental property.

      2. In terms of pain, although we can say that an activity in relevant areas of the brain causally brings about a specific mental property, namely, intensity of pain, we still have the problem of accounting for how it is that the experience (sensation) of pain causes a bodily reaction, such as moving our hand away from fire.

      3. Moreover, many of our self-protective reactions take place at the level of reflexes and require no consciousness whatever, let alone a definite "experience."

   B. Thoughts are philosophically referred to as "intentional objects," meaning the tendency of all mental acts toward an object.

      1. This *intentionality* is of central importance to our consideration of mental causation.

      2. The philosopher/psychologist Franz Brentano (1838–1917) pointed out that whether the activity is that of perceiving, desiring, remembering, feeling, knowing, or intending, it is always *about* something.

      3. Brentano drew a sharp line between the mental and the physical. The latter is never *about* something.

      4. How can any physical feature or property give rise to the "aboutness" of thoughts, feelings, and so on? How do mental events, which are about something, causally bring about physical events lacking in this very property?

   C. Some philosophers have suggested that we should content ourselves with ordinary forms of explanation.

      1. The philosopher Georges Rey suggests that problems be divided into those "peculiar to the mind" and those outside the mind.

      2. This fits the notion of customary explanations as containing the "causal" conditions within themselves.

3. But the central task of any discipline, once it has mapped out its territory, is to arrive at a settled position on just how far its explanatory resources are likely to take it.
4. In philosophy of mind, to raise the question of mental causation moves the philosophical question to a scientific question.
5. Is it any surprise that the philosopher asking what is, at base, a scientific question, soon discovers the inability of philosophical modes of explanation to settle it?

III. It can be argued that questions of causation are, in principle and always, scientific questions. Furthermore, much of what we do in our daily lives is not best understood in causal terms.
  A. Much of what we do in the ordinary affairs of life we have a reason for doing, reason being understood in a fairly broad sense—the person acting has some end or goal in mind.
    1. The primary antecedent conditions for actions are reasons.
    2. When viewed at a metaphysically safe distance, it would seem quite hard to ask how a reason for acting causes the action that is intelligibly related to it.
    3. To act for a reason is to engage the larger world. The action is tied to an understanding of the surrounding environment and what it affords by way of possibilities for acting.
    4. Having the same reason but finding oneself in a radically different environment might call for radically different courses of action.
    5. Thus, causal accounts, drawn from the much more orderly world of physical objects in motion, prove to be far too limited when we attempt to bring them into the world of real life as actually lived.
  B. Are causes and reasons fundamentally different?
    1. Mustn't reasons be a species of cause if reasons are able to bring actions about?
    2. To require this connection is to adopt the very physicalistic perspective that a "reasons" account challenges.
    3. As of now, we are strongly inclined to regard all instances of motion and activity as candidates for explanations based on physical causes. That position

could be called metaphysically "correct," but it could also be false.

4. Despite the tremendous growth of knowledge over recent decades, the problem of mental causation, nonetheless, is pretty much where it was in the time of the ancient Greek philosophers.

Essential Reading:

Heil, John, and Alfred Mele, eds., *Mental Causation.*

Supplementary Reading:

Kim, J., "Mental Causation and Consciousness: The Two Mind-Body Problems for the Physicalist," in *Physicalism and Its Discontents.*

Questions to Consider:

1. What is a "cause"?

2. We enter a room, flip a switch, and light floods the room. What would enter into a complete "causal" account of this occurrence?

Lecture Five—Transcript
Mental Causation

In the previous lecture I addressed the question of the nature of the relationship between mental and physical events that might be plausibly defended in attempts to close the explanatory gap. I noted then that causal relationships are serious candidates, but that these also face serious problems. It is customary to expect in any causal relationship that the antecedent-consequent events—or, as we might say, causes and effects—will be of a kindred sort.

The stock example is that of two billiard balls colliding. We're prepared to accept action at a distance, such as the effect of the moon's gravitational field on earthly tides. But the moon is a big object, not too far away in astrological distance. It would be expected to have the same sort of effect on water that gravitational fields have on other kinds of physical bodies. In other words, although one might think of gravitational effects as representing or illustrating action at a distance, it's an action that takes place between two indisputably physical bodies.

Can the same be said of mental causation? Does my desire and my decision to raise my arm *cause* my arm to be raised? If so, am I to understand this causal relationship as one that obtains between, on one side of the cause-effect relation, a massless, spaceless, mental event; and, on the other side, the movement of a physical mass from one location to another?

At a common sense level, one is likely to be perplexed by the claim that mental causes pose a serious problem. What could be more obvious than that the things we think about have the power to bring about the things we choose to do? Philip decides that it's too hot for hot chocolate and proceeds to fix himself an ice tea. If we observe Philip as he proceeds to boil water, take tea bags from the cupboard, slice the lemons, and carry the sugar bowl to the table where he has placed a tall glass, we have no doubt about what he's doing and we have no doubt but that he planned all this—as we might say—"in his mind" prior to moving himself and his limbs in ways that would bring this all about. Now, the only alternative explanation would be that we're watching someone in a sleepwalk.

Now, all this pertains to third-person accounts; that is, accounts where we're watching the behavior of someone else and making inferences about what might be going on in that person's mind. The first-person account is transparently simple: I decided that it's too hot for hot chocolate, and I proceed to make myself a glass of ice tea. Now, unless I'm suffering from some serious neurological or psychiatric disorder, the question will never occur to me as to whether what I'm doing was planned and governed by my own mind. If I asked why I was doing these things, I would reply that I had decided to have ice tea. I'd think it quite odd if I were then asked how such a decision could actually make parts of my body move.

Again, except under conditions of illness, our actions quite faithfully follow our decisions, and our decisions are quite clearly not material objects. At the commonsense level, and in the ordinary affairs of life, we simply take for granted that the plans and purposes shaped within our own mental life causally bring about actions capable of realizing those very plans and purposes.

Considered philosophically, however, this state of affairs is highly perplexing. And considered scientifically, it seems virtually nearly impossible. What the commonsense account requires is for something mental—which is to say something immaterial—to set in motion large muscle masses and large skeletal frames, and to guide these through complex, delicate, and coordinated series of movements.

One option available to us, if we seek to get out of this bind, is simply to attach ourselves to a form of physicalism and insist that decisions, judgments, plans, and purposes are simply code words. For what? For physical events in the brain. There are several factors that make this less than an appealing option.

If we were to set about to recast all statements that we've customarily made about our plans and purposes, our decisions and judgments, into physicalistic language, our statements would be essentially unintelligible to others. Indeed, they'd probably be unintelligible to us even as we uttered the sentences. Presumably we could learn how to translate these physicalistic terms back into the vernacular language, but little would be gained in that case, because the meaningfulness of the utterances would be tied to the very language that, for some reason, we had abandoned in the first place. The entire enterprise would be a nightmare.

Think of lining up all the characteristics of physical events and physical objects in the left-hand column of some huge spreadsheet. Now put all of the characteristics of mental events in the right hand column. And now think of attempting to match something in the left-hand column with such entries on the right as decision making, judgments of duty, longing for a peaceful life, wanting a chocolate ice cream cone, believing it will be a rainy spring—the matches simply fall apart. Nothing plausibly matches at all.

Undaunted, many philosophers have attempted to have their cake and eat it too. Donald Davidson, for example, has long defended the thesis that he labeled *anomalous monism.* Davidson adopts a monistic ontology, which he regards as consistent with the most advanced thinking in science. On this account, there's only one kind of stuff in reality, and that is physical stuff. Nevertheless, the events and processes that we've traditionally regarded as our mental life are not reducible or directly translatable into physical terms and concepts. Here, then, is the anomaly.

On Davidson's account, mental events and processes do bring about physical events in just the sense of strict causation. To do this, they must themselves be physical, but of such a nature as to preclude reduction to the terms of the physical sciences. This is anomalous, for we are required to retain a dualistic vocabulary even as we acknowledge a monistic reality. Hence, anomalous monism.

Well, perhaps the most obvious criticism of this view is that it permits the very mental properties that make the causal model problematical in the first place. If Davidson is willing to include mental properties and, at the same time, regard them as irreducible to physical properties, then one has to have an answer to the question, "How did these mental properties—these actually veiled physical properties—get caused by the non-veiled physical properties of the brain?"

It's interesting that Davidson resists the very notion of properties as such, and also resists the conventional view that one thing causes another through some sort of causal mechanism or process requiring identification. Instead, Davidson takes the position that where there is causation, one thing causes another by just causing it.

Now, Davidson, I should note, is not alone in his skepticism regarding properties. Some philosophers have argued that properties are themselves simply ensembles of causes. Thus, when we say that water is a universal solvent, we are saying that it causes things to dissolve. So the right inventory of properties on this account is just an inventory of the observed effects things have on other things.

How interesting! Well, at this point it might be timely to consider further just what we mean by properties. What is a mental property, for example? I have rather more confidence in answering questions about physical properties, for one might just list such features of an object as its weight, height, shape, hardness, etc. However, none of these could be meaningfully applied to anything we're inclined to regard as mental; only metaphorically would we refer to the *shape* of an argument, or the *hardness* of one's position, or the *height* of folly or of humor, or of humor that is *off-color*.

Before we can prepare any sort of a list of mental properties, we have to be clear as to what we mean by mental contents in the first place; or just mental entities. For some X to have properties, there must be an X. For the garden gate to have properties, there must be a garden gate. For there to be mental properties, there must be something mental. What might the mental items be, which in some way bear certain properties?

Perhaps the most obvious ones are experiences and thoughts. By experiences, I refer to our perceptions. When I perceive a red rose I could say, in a somewhat cumbersome fashion, that I am having the experience associated with the perception of a red rose; or an experience of the sort normally brought about when I am looking at a red rose under proper conditions of illumination and with a visual system that is functioning in a proper way. I'm not sure about how to convert all of this into a mental property, however, for surely in perceiving a red rose I'm not having a red experience or a red idea. Rather, I am recording one of the objective facts of the object in front of me; namely, that it's red. In this case, the property of redness is assigned to the rose, not to the mental activity or the perception.

Suppose instead the experience is that of pain. Again, it would seem to be unnecessary and somewhat distracting to say something like, "I am having the experience of a toothache." It's generally sufficient to say, "I have a toothache." We're all familiar with aches and pains. Except in the philosophy literature, however, these are not regarded as mental events, but as unpleasant sensations occurring in various regions of one's body.

In the matter of certain pains, the neurophysiological details have been fairly accurately, even completely, worked out. Heightened activity in the unmyelinated c-fibers in sensory nerves are reliably associated with reported pain. As the signals are transmitted to regions of the brain, it is even possible to block them physically and, thus, avert a pain that would otherwise naturally occur. The relationship is so reliable, here, that, by the usual standards, we seem to be on sure footing in saying that discharges in the c-fibers and resulting activity in specific regions of the brain causally bring about pain. We might go further and say that a relationship obtains between the degree of activity in the relevant areas of the brain and the intensity of the pain.

Now, the intensity of pain is one of its properties. To that extent, we can say that a specific physical property—namely, activity in the relevant areas of the brain—causally brings about a specific mental property—namely, intensity of pain. Let us go a step further and record the reliable relationship between the presence of intense pain and the rapid movement of one's hand away from the flame. At this point, at least in principle, we have a rich catalog of pain properties and a comparable catalog of neurophysiological events reliably related to these.

But how does this, or any similar observation, settle the problem we began with; namely, the problem of mental causation? We still have the problem of accounting for how it is that a given physical property causes the experience of pain: the problem of accounting for how it is that the experience of pain—the sensation—the mental event, so to speak, causes the hand to be withdrawn.

When we think about this further, yet another question arises, not unlike questions we confronted in connection with zombies in the first lecture in this series. From a design point of view, it should be quite easy to construct a device that moves away from sources of stimulation that have a destructive effect on it or any part of it. It's not at all clear that the experience of pain adds much by way of survival value. After all, many of our self-protective reactions take place at the level of reflexes and require no consciousness whatever, let alone a definite experience. Is it not just excess baggage adding conscious experience to all the apparatus already sufficient to produce self-protective behavior? I'll not consider this question just yet.

©2007 The Teaching Company.

Let me turn instead to still another class of mental events; in this case, thoughts. All thought is thought about something, by which I mean that thought has content. What we think about need not have real existence, of course. For several centuries, the European hierarchy set out to identify, prosecute, and even execute witches, thinking them to be heretics. We must assume that many officials at the time were obsessed with thoughts of witches; though, as it happens, there simply aren't actual witches. Again, that thought has content is not to say that such content is invariably real.

There is a somewhat misleading term in philosophy for the contents of thought, for what thoughts are about; they are referred to as *intentional objects*—here, meaning not the specific intention to do something, but the tendency of all mental acts toward an object. When the watchman claims he saw a witch flying over the church steeple, we need a term for what was seen. As there was no witch, and therefore, none flying over the steeple, we say that in this instance the witch was an intentional object in the watchman's mind or thought.

This intentionality is of central importance to our consideration of mental causation. The term itself has medieval roots in its philosophical heritage. The Latin *intentio* in scholastic philosophy refers to one's conception of something, which may or may not match up with reality. In more modern times, it was the philosopher-psychologist Franz Brentano who drew attention to one of the identifying features of what we have been referring to as the mental. Whether the activity is that of perceiving, desiring, remembering, feeling, knowing, believing, or intending, it is always *about* something. It is the "aboutness" of these mental activities that is so special. Brentano put it this way:

> Every mental phenomenon includes something as object within itself, although they do not do so in the same way. In presentation, something is presented, in judgment something is affirmed or denied, in love loved, in hate hated, in desire desired and so on. … This intentional inexistence is characteristic exclusively of mental phenomena. No physical phenomenon exhibits anything like it. We can, therefore, define mental phenomena by saying that they are those phenomena which contain an object intentionally within themselves.

Brentano draws the sharp dividing line between all that is mental and all that is physical. The former is always about something, and the latter never is. Could a dichotomy be any sharper? Sodium chloride is salt, but it isn't about anything. "That tastes salty" is about something; it's about what I'm tasting. There are no desires without content; nor are there hopes without something for which we hope; nor is there knowledge, except that which knowledge is about. In these and kindred cases, what is presupposed is one who knows, one who hopes, one who feels, one who thinks, one who is experiencing something.

Now, let us be clear on what this dichotomy seems to indicate about the issue of mental causation. If the objects of mental events are intentional objects—which is to say, if the objects of mental events are always about something—whereas physical objects do not have this feature or property, we are then left with the question of how any physical feature or property could give rise to the very *aboutness* of thoughts, feelings, knowledge, etc.

Similarly, the question arises as to how mental events, which are about something, causally bring about events that are physical and utterly lacking in this very property.

Now, let me not be overly metaphysical on this point. I mean only to raise a question about the extent to which causally related objects and events would be expected—what sort of relationship we'd expect them to have, and that would be least one property in common between them. The common property may not be as obvious as the comparable masses of two billiard balls; but there should be something, if only something spatio-temporal, shared by causes and their effects.

Is it possible that in these respects, we're really are asking for too much? Some have suggested that causal explanations are of a rather exotic sort, and that we might just content ourselves with ordinary forms of explanation. When we say that objects fall toward the center of the earth because they're under the influence of gravitational forces, we take that to be an explanation. Now, to press on and ask further, "Well, just what it is in gravity that is the source of this force?" would lead to an infinite regress. Let's say that the source of gravitational forces is something called a *graviton*. Well, then we'd have to ask what it is about gravitons that have them create effects of the sort we've observed, ad infinitum.

About a decade ago, the philosopher George Rey set down an interesting maxim in a book devoted to philosophy of mind. He called it a fairness maxim and he expressed it in these words:

> Don't burden the mind with everyone else's problems. Always ask whether a problem is peculiar to the mind, or whether the issue could equally well be raised in other less problematic areas. If it can be, settle it for those areas first, and then assess the philosophy of mind.

Well, this ties in nicely with the notion of customary explanations as containing the causal conditions within themselves. When I say that Nick drove to the store to buy a quart of milk, it would be odd if someone then asked me by what mechanism all this was brought about. And, in fact, it would be impossible to provide a completely causal account of everything that had to be accomplished. Except for the metaphysically cranky, most would accept the proposition that the causal account is just included in the statement that Nick drove to the store *to buy* a quart of milk. And if I say that, as a result of Mary's thirst, she went to the fridge and *poured* a glass of milk, most native speakers will understand that the cause of Mary going to the fridge was her thirst.

Some will regard this approach as nothing less than philosophical surrender. Critics might say that a strategy of this sort would conveniently solve all the problems that philosophy is ever likely to confront. Present a problem, and the solution is to insist that, that's just the way things are.

But I do think this misses the point. The central task of any discipline, once it has mapped out its territory, it is to arrive at a settled position on just how far its explanatory resources are likely to take it. To stretch these resources beyond their intrinsic powers is actually to abandon the discipline itself and perhaps to enter another, and quite different, discipline.

This has become all too apparent within philosophy of mind. In raising the very question of mental causation, the philosopher has moved from a philosophical question to a scientific question, though it may be as intractable in science as it proved to be in philosophy. Is it any surprise that the philosopher asking what at base is a scientific question soon discovers the inability of philosophical modes of explanation to settle it?

In the present context, I would submit that questions of causation are in principle and always scientific questions. But I would go further than this. I would say that much of what we do in the ordinary affairs of life is not to be understood in causal terms; much of what we do in the ordinary affairs of life, we have a reason for doing.

I would have the concept of reasons here understood fairly broadly. By having a reason, I submit that the person acting has some end or goal in mind; some set of rational desires and motives; some condition or state of need calling for a particular course of action. Having a reason to act generally brings about an action. The actual record of human activities, since the time such records have been kept, leaves no doubt at all, but that the primary antecedent conditions for actions are reasons. We have well-developed psychiatric categories for persons whose actions bear no intelligible connection to the reasons they claim to be moved by; or for that matter to any reasons at all!

Needless to say, there is much work to be done both in psychology and in philosophy on the question of just how reasons and actions match up. When viewed at a metaphysically safe distance, however, it would seem strange to ask just how a reason for acting *causes* the actions intelligibly related to it.

There is still more to say about all this. To act for a reason or to act with a reason is to engage the larger world; indeed, it is to see the world in a certain aspect. The action now is tied to an understanding of the surrounding environment and what it affords by way of possibilities for acting. Having the same reason, but finding oneself in a radically different environment, might call for radically different courses of action. Having nothing but a shopping bag and finding oneself in the middle of a rainstorm may lead to the shopping bag now converted to a makeshift umbrella. The point I wish to make here is that causal accounts, drawn from the much more orderly world of physical objects in motion, soon prove to be far too thin and far too limited when we attempt to bring them into the busy, cluttered, noisy, sometimes unfathomable world of real life, as actually lived.

Are causes and reasons fundamentally different? Mustn't reasons be a species of cause, if reasons are able to bring about actions? To require such a connection, however, is to adopt the very physicalistic perspective that a "reasons" account challenges. As of now, we are strongly inclined to regard all instances of motion and activity as candidates for explanations based on physical causes. Some might say that this is the metaphysically correct assumption. However, it may also be false.

There will always be more to learn about the nervous system, I am sure; but we do know a great deal. I would go so far as to say that 90% of what we know has been learned in the course of my own lifetime. This impressive growth of knowledge, nonetheless, has left the problem of mental causation pretty much where it was in the time of the ancient Greek philosophers. I do not offer this observation to justify total surrender. It should, however, have something of a chastening effect on those who insist that the problem of mental causation is just a technical problem, ultimately to be settled through scientific progress and the proper application of experimental methods.

As for the claim that we know very little about causality in any area, and, therefore, should not expect much more when it comes to mental life, I would submit that ignorance in one domain may be based on factors quite different from the ignorance we suffer in a quite different domain. To say that my friend is ignorant of the birthday present I've bought for him, is to say something different from my friend being ignorant as to how his desires cause his body to move. The first form of ignorance will be removed by a fact, and that fact will appear sometime on the day of his birthday. As of now, there is no compelling reason to believe that some set of facts will remove that second kind of ignorance on any birthday. We stay tuned, of course, even during long periods of static!

Well, as if all this were not vexing enough, consider the basis upon which we have any right to conclude that there are minds other than our own. Well, are there other minds? Tune in next time.

Lecture Six
Other Minds

Scope:

The problem of how we know there are other minds than our own is part of the epistemological problem of how it is that I know anything. It is more than a linguistic problem, as we shall see in this lecture, when we explore the positions taken by Ludwig Wittgenstein and the Scottish philosopher Thomas Reid, who countered skepticism with a pragmatic approach to the problem of other minds.

Outline

I. At the heart of a certain form of skepticism, known as *solipsism*, is the question: How do I know there are any minds other than my own?

   A. A solipsist is prepared to make no claim other than the fact of his own existence and mental life. The problem of other minds, then, is just the problem of answering the solipsist.

   B. In one sense, the problem of other minds is cut from the same cloth as all fundamental problems in epistemology: Basically, the problem of other minds is just part of the problem of how it is that I know anything or can claim that I know something.

      1. I can perceive that I have a mind, but I cannot perceive any mind other than my own.

      2. Even if an apparatus existed that could show us an image of another mind, another mind in a conscious state associated with pain, for example, we would have no knowledge of the pain as actually felt.

   C. Ludwig Wittgenstein (1889–1951) held that language may not be a reliable guide to correctly interpreting the statements of another, as any two persons may associate two different meanings with a single word.

II. But the problem of other minds is surely not merely a linguistic problem.

   A. The problem of other minds may be seen to arise once we attach all of our knowledge claims to direct perception.

B. It is an evidentiary problem, in the sense that it becomes "problematical" only when we use the wrong sort of evidence.

C. If direct perception constitutes the only justification for claiming to know anything, then, in fact, whole realms of what we regard as the "known" become quite obscure.

    1. I do not directly perceive such laws as the laws of the internal combustion engine; my belief in them is inferential.

    2. If I were a scientist, my belief would be based on the developed conception of the lawfulness of nature itself, namely, that if such laws were not persistent over time, the very coherence of the cosmos would be dissolved.

    3. Little of such abstract reasoning is available at the level of direct perception.

D. It could be argued, however, that to talk of the "coherence of the cosmos" simply reflects another of our prejudices.

    1. A "coherent cosmos" can arguably be thought of as just one of an infinitely large number of pictures that might be drawn to capture the nature of reality.

    2. This sort of question is at the heart of a contemporary issue within philosophy of science that is usually categorized as "realism versus antirealism."

    3. Do our scientific laws really express "reality"?

III. The *pragmatic* ground is one particular ground of justification for knowledge claims of any sort.

A. A pragmatic ground belongs to a class of assumptions or dispositions absent which the very conduct of life would become nearly impossible.

B. The 18th-century Scottish philosopher Thomas Reid (1710–1796) advanced commonsense arguments against the seemingly impregnable position of the skeptic.

    1. Reid held that we do not enter the world with utterly blank slates by way of our psychological or mental resources; instinct and intuition are natural endowments, supplemented by perception and learning.

    2. For Reid, if the rich resources of perception are to serve their own purposes, they must not be nullified by the philosophical pretensions of the skeptic.

C. On the problem of other minds, Reid argued that while we cannot directly perceive any other mind external to our own, we do perceive the behavior of others.
   1. On Reid's understanding, the possibility of any form of social interaction presupposes certain instinctual patterns of behavior.
   2. The meaning of these patterns will be understood by members of that species, even across species.

D. To briefly summarize Reid's position on language, we begin with John Locke's theory, which we can take as the conventional position on the manner in which words come to have meaning.
   1. According to Locke, and many others, a pattern of sound becomes meaningful as speech when language users accept it as such.
   2. Reid was perhaps the first to recognize that this account will not work. In order for there to be agreements, there must be some language in place by which to establish them.
   3. Reid distinguished between what he called *natural* language and the language we speak, which he dubbed *artificial* language.
   4. Natural language refers to body language and intonation and is recognizable across species. In the prelinguistic world of primitive man, it served as a support for the development of artificial language.
   5. As with other natural endowments, there is no rational justification for judging the signs and symbols of natural language.

E. Reid held the problem of other minds to be analogous to his concept of language: When other creatures express themselves in a manner comparable to our own natural expressions of our emotions and desires, we are led insensibly to the belief that they, too, have a mental life that includes just these emotions and desires.

IV. To the extent that Reid's argument is from analogy, it faces philosophical and conceptual objections.

A. Norman Malcolm (1911–1990) argued that because an individual's own mental states and behavior are confined to one person, this affords no grounds for a generalization to any other person.

1. Malcolm's argument, however, can be seen as inadequate.
2. There may be a confusion as to just what is being generalized.
3. The generalization does not proceed from one mind to all other minds but from a very large number of correlated mental states and behavioral expressions.
4. In the course of a day, each one of us has thousands of correlated mental states and behavioral expressions on which to ground our "generalizations."

B. What Reid refers to as natural language is very close to Wittgenstein's notion of natural expressions; certain natural expressions constitute a warrant for believing that someone else is happy, in pain, and so on.

C. Clearly, our recognition of other minds constitutes the basis of one of the most important ingredients of social life: empathy.

D. Both our conduct toward others and what we expect from them depend to a considerable extent on our ability to project ourselves into their situation.

E. We may tentatively conclude that nature fits both humans and nonhumans with certain basic tendencies and dispositions such that we are able to adjust to significant environmental impositions without having to learn how to cope with everything.

Essential Reading:

Avramides, A., *Other Minds*.

Questions to Consider:

1. Your best friend happens to be a state-of-the-art robot. How can you tell?
2. Some psychiatric patients present themselves as having multiple personalities. Is this evidence of multiple "minds" in one body?

Lecture Six—Transcript
Other Minds

The topic of this sixth lecture is "Other Minds." The key question is a straightforward one: How do I know there are any minds other than my own? This question is at the heart of a certain form of skepticism, known as solipsism. The solipsist is prepared to make no claim other than the facts of his own existence and mental life, satisfied that the only reality is that which is minted within the utterly private duchy of his own consciousness. The problem of other minds, then, is just the problem of answering the solipsist.

Now, in one sense, this problem is cut from the same cloth as all fundamental problems in epistemology. At base, the problem of other minds is just part of the problem of how it is we are justified in claiming to know anything.

Let us say, at least for the sake of argument, that I know that I have a mind, owing to the direct and immediate access that I have to my own mental states. I might even say that the basis of this knowledge is not unlike the foundation of all my knowledge claims; namely, direct perception. By way of introspection, I am able to perceive—in a manner of speaking—the events, states, and contents of my own mind.

But here, we then come face-to-face with the problem of other minds. It's plainly the case that I cannot perceive any mind other than my own. Of course, strictly speaking, we cannot perceive our own minds, either; for to do so it would be necessary for the mind to be some sort of perceptible object.

Let's just say—speaking loosely at this point—that I'm aware of certain thoughts, experiences, and feelings as being my own; and that, for convenience, I say that these are part of my mental life. Thus, I say that I am aware that I have a mind, at least in this loose sense. But I do not have direct awareness of the thoughts, experiences, and feelings of anyone else. I have no database, therefore, with which to justify my imputing mind to anyone but myself.

Note, however, that, even if I had access to such data, there would still be the problem of other minds if the access were not of the first-person variety. Let me illustrate the point with a thought-experiment. Let us say that we have a television picture of events occurring inside the skull of Mrs. Smith—these being allegedly mental events. The apparatus is such that, when the screen turns green, Mrs. Smith reports hearing sounds and seeing objects. Now, even if we had an arrangement such as this, the problem of other minds would persist; for all I would be able to say, when the green light is on, is that this signals certain verbal behavior on the part of Mrs. Smith. I would not know for certain whether she was conscious, or aware; nor would I know just what the contents of her consciousness might be. For all I know, she might be a well-constructed robot with a tape recorder that's activated by green light.

Well, let's add ever more sensitive equipment such that, in addition to the green light, there are various symbols displayed indicating certain stimuli, which would cause me to have a pain, and that these are now being delivered to Mrs. Smith. Yet other symbols arise, which, were they recorded from me, would be associated with my experiencing an itchy chin, or the sound of a barn owl, or the aroma of freshly brewed coffee. Again, even with all this, I would be under no obligation to accept that there is actually another mind, a mind distinct from my own. All such data from Mrs. Smith could be no more than a kind of computer printout, providing a record of certain input-output relations. I could not be sure that Mrs. Smith has a mind, or that she is in some sort of mental state, or that she is experiencing coffee, pain, or anything at all.

Our thought-experiment permits us to see another side of the issue. Consider how such an apparatus might have been constructed in the first place. We would have some means by which to sample and measure accurately the events taking place in many regions within the brain. All this would be accomplished with a fully conscious subject. Computer programs would be written to keep track of the verbal reports of each subject, and the states of the brain associated with each of those reports. With a large enough set of correlations, we could improve our ability to match a particular event in the brain with a particular subjective state, as reported by a given subject.

Now, all this having been done, we now have our colleague Samantha tied into the system. At first, Samantha was going to cancel the appointment. She told us she had been having some trouble with one of her teeth. Gamely, however, she has agreed to participate. It is under these conditions that the equipment reports not only that Samantha is conscious, but that she is in pain. Again, we might be willing to accept that she is conscious and in pain, but we must still admit that we have no direct knowledge of any of this.

That I have an itch is known by me directly; that you have an itch is something I can only infer from certain behavior on your part, including verbal behavior.

Well, one might wish to take a commonsense position here and declare straightaway, that if I say I have a toothache, and Samantha says that she has a toothache, we know what each other means, and that's the end of it! But, that things are not this simple is illustrated by a passage from Ludwig Wittgenstein's *Philosophical Investigations*, "You surely know what "It is 5 o'clock here" means; so you also know what "It's 5 o'clock on the sun" means. It means simply that it is the same time there as it is here when it is 5 o'clock." He's being whimsical.

The point here is that the persons using these words are possibly as far apart in the sense in which they are using the words as might be the conditions prevailing on earth, and on the surface of the sun. In the absence of a very careful analysis of the basis upon which such terms are used, there's simply no way of knowing whether the two persons are referring to anything at all, let alone to two versions of the same thing.

I should stay with Wittgenstein for a moment, and his famous "beetle in a box." It's a way of illustrating the problem. Imagine a half-dozen people, each holding a small box. Each person can see what is inside the box he is holding, but can't see inside any other box. Suppose when queried, each of them takes a peek, and reports that what's inside his or her box is, "a beetle!" Unless we are sure that all of the participants are members of the same *language game*—one of Wittgenstein's terms—we have no way of knowing what the utterance *beetle* refers to. One of the participants might be from a distant planet where the utterance *beetle* refers to a stone. Yet another participant might come from a linguistic community in which *beetle* is the term for *empty*. In all, then, it is insufficient, as regards the problem of other minds, to know no more than that two people are using the same words.

Many might regard Wittgenstein's strictures here as overdrawn. As it happens, we have the same information regarding the linguistic conventions of those with whom we share such conversations as we do when we see how they are dressed, how they generally comport themselves, etc. All I should want to say at this point is that, however the problem of other minds is to be understood, it's surely not merely a linguistic problem. At base, I submit that the problem of other minds arises once we attach all of our knowledge claims to direct perception. As I shall try to show with the help of Thomas Reid, it is an evidentiary problem, in the sense that it becomes problematical only when we use the wrong sort of evidence.

To make this clear, let me begin with direct perception. If direct perception constitutes the only justification for claiming to know anything; then, in fact, whole realms of what we regard as the known become quite obscure. Within limits, I am confident that when I turn the ignition key on tomorrow morning, the engine in my automobile will start up. My confidence is based on the belief that the laws governing the internal combustion engine continue to be valid over time, and were not suspended last night. Thus, if the car doesn't start tomorrow morning, I do not become skeptical about the persistence of the laws of the internal combustion engine; rather, I arrange to have the car serviced. Nonetheless, I never directly perceive a law. In matters of this sort, my belief is entirely inferential. It's a generalization based on past experience.

If I'm a scientist, however, my belief is based on something far more substantial than past experience. It's based on the developed conception of the lawfulness of nature itself. I can put this more grandly. It's based on the conviction that if laws such as those governing the internal combustion engine were not persistent over time, the very coherence of the cosmos would be dissolved. The scientific position is based here on whole clusters of abstract reasoning, little of it available at the level of direct perception. Indeed, it is based on certain abstract mathematical precepts that are forever beyond the reach of perception.

Of course, referring to something like *coherence of the cosmos* seems to beg the very question at issue. Who says the cosmos is coherent? Is such a perspective not simply another of our prejudices? Is it not just one of an indefinitely large number of pictures that might be drawn to capture the nature of reality? Questions of this sort are at the very heart of a contemporary issue within philosophy of science, usually subsumed under the heading, "Realism versus Anti-realism." Do the laws of science express what is really the case in the cosmos, or are they merely shorthand summaries of experiences we've had under conditions of highly controlled observation? Do our scientific laws express reality in the full, most faithful sense?

Well, our plate is full enough without my attempting to answer this question! Those who defend a realist position, however, would be inclined to say that the success of such extraordinary projects as the space program (which I mentioned in an earlier lecture) would be utterly inexplicable, except on the assumption that the laws on which that program is based are true. Now, I bring this up in order to present one particular ground of justification for knowledge claims of any sort. It is the *pragmatic* ground.

I hope not to be misunderstood here. The pragmatism I'm prepared to defend is not captured by such trendy expressions as, "If it works, it must be true." I refer instead to a class of assumptions or dispositions, absent which, the very conduct of life, including philosophical life, would become nearly impossible. My guide here, as I mentioned, is the 18th century Scottish philosopher, Thomas Reid. My Oxford colleague, Anita Avramides, in her excellent book on other minds, argues that Reid was surely among the first philosophers to recognize the problem of other minds in its modern form.

A relentless critic of skepticism, Reid advanced commonsense arguments against the seemingly impregnable position of the skeptic. Consider this passage from Reid's work, *An Inquiry into the Human Mind:*

> The skeptic asks me, Why do you believe the existence of the external object which you perceive? This belief, sir, is none of my manufacture; it came from the mint of Nature; it bears her image and superscription; and, if it is not right, the fault is not mine: I even took it upon trust, and without suspicion. Reason, says the skeptic, is the only judge of truth, and you ought to throw off every opinion and every belief that is not grounded on reason. Why, sir, should I believe the faculty of reason more than that of perception?— they both came out of the same shop, and were made by the same artist; and if he puts one piece of false ware into my hands, what should hinder him from putting another?

Reid's rejoinder takes for granted that we do not enter the world with utterly blank slates by way of our psychological or mental resources. The animal kingdom displays numerous and diverse patterns of behavior that are instinctual and that protect and promote life long before the animals could possibly learn such behavior. The caterpillar crawling over countless leaves, says Reid, till reaching the one that's right for its own physiology, does so not with the knowledge of a scientist, but under the undeliberated guidance of a surer authority. Instinct and intuition are natural endowments, in place to be supplemented by perception and learning. But if the rich resources of perception are to serve their own purposes, they must not be nullified by the philosophical pretensions of the skeptic.

Now, let's listen to Thomas Reid again on just this point:

> No man seeks a reason for believing what he sees or feels; and, if he did, it would be difficult to find one. But, though he can give no reason for believing his senses, his belief remains as firm as if it were grounded on demonstration. Many eminent philosophers, thinking it unreasonable to believe when they could not shew a reason, have laboured to furnish us with reasons for believing our senses; but their reasons are very insufficient, and will not bear examination. Other philosophers have shewn very clearly the fallacy of these reasons, and have, as they imagine, discovered invincible reasons against this belief; but they have never been able either to shake it themselves or to convince others. The statesman continues to plod, the soldier to fight, and the merchant to export and import, without being in the least moved by the demonstrations that have been offered of the non-existence of those things about which they are so seriously employed. And a man may as soon by reasoning, pull the moon out of her orbit, as destroy the belief of the objects of sense.

Let me now apply Reid's perspective to the problem of other minds. Of course we cannot directly perceive any other mind—any mind external to our own. We do, however, perceive the behavior of others. On Reid's understanding, the very possibility of any form of social interaction at all presupposes certain instinctual patterns of behavior, the meaning of which will be understood by members of that species; in fact, understood across species. As Reid says, "the first time one sees a stern and fierce look, a contracted brow…a menacing posture, he concludes that the person is inflamed with anger."

Let me take a step back from this and briefly summarize Thomas Reid's position on language. Toward the end of the 17th century, John Locke gave added weight to the traditional view that words derive their meaning solely by use and by convention, such that all language is governed by social rules and local practices. According to Locke, and many others, a pattern of sound becomes meaningful as speech when language users accept it as such. The object I'm speaking into is called a microphone, not because the pattern of sound, *microphone,* in any way matches the physical properties of the object itself. Rather, by convention, the English-speaking world has given objects of this kind the generic name, *microphone.* The meaning of the word is nothing other than conventional agreements as to how it is to be used, or as to what it represents.

Now, Reid was perhaps the first to recognize that this account simply will not work; for, in order for there to be agreements, covenants, or conventions of any kind at all, *they* must depend on some language—some language that must be in place by which to establish and signal agreement. We cannot agree to call some object a microphone, unless we have some means by which to signal our agreement.

Reid distinguished between what he called *natural language* and the language that I am now speaking, which he dubs *artificial language.* The term *natural language* refers to modes of expression that are naturally or instinctually endowed. These are in the form of grimaces, posture, and intonation. Reid regards these as widely distributed in the animal kingdom, and in fact, functional across species. We readily recognize the difference between an angry dog and a friendly one.

If there ever was to be cooperative behavior between and among human beings, there must have been some basis in the prelinguistic world of primitive man, by which persons could signal basic sentiments and desires. There must have been a natural language by which to record agreement. Only in this way could an artificial language be developed, which then, conventionally, would have terms come to represent specific things.

Natural language, then, becomes a kind of scaffolding, on which the artificial language might be grafted. As with other natural endowments, there is no rational justification or argument according to which the signs and symbols of a natural language are to be judged. They are not to be judged at all; they are to be used; and it is their role in actual practice that establishes their validity.

Even with the intellectual bounty conferred by artificial language, our day-to-day affairs and communications are still surprisingly marked by the infusion of natural language. Anger is often accompanied by a rigidity of posture, an increase in the volume of one's voice. The joy that we feel very often expresses itself in the form of smiles. Sadness, too, is revealed through characteristic facial expressions and body postures. Charles Darwin was attentive to these aspects of natural language and, in fact, systematically recorded how the emotions of animals, including human animals, are expressed facially, vocally, and posturally.

In light of all this, it should be clear how Thomas Reid deals with the problem of other minds. At the most primitive level, the behavior of creatures that at least look like ourselves comes to be the basis upon which we judge the conditions giving rise to that behavior. Where such creatures express themselves in a manner comparable to our own natural expressions of emotions and desires, we are led insensibly to the belief that they, too, have a mental life that includes just these emotions and desires. It is not that we're unable to adopt a skeptical position toward this. It is, instead, that were we to act on this skepticism, the possibility of significant interactions with other creatures would be reduced to a nullity. Nor is it the case that in adopting one or another position, we deliberate at the level of pragmatics. The position we take is not based on deliberation. It is based instead on the strongest of natural inclinations, absent which, life within society would be virtually impossible.

To the extent that Thomas Reid's argument is an argument from analogy, it faces serious philosophical and conceptual objections. One of these was developed years ago by Norman Malcolm. At base, the challenge goes like this: The analogical argument is inferential; it is in the form of a generalization from the relationship between my mental states and behavior to the mental states and behavior of another. But my mental states and behavior are confined solely to one person, and this affords no ground whatever for a generalization to any other, let alone to all others.

I must say, this does not seem to be a fatal objection, and it may be based on a confusion as to just what is being generalized. The generalization does not proceed from one mind to all other minds, but from a very large number of correlated mental states and behavioral expressions. In the course of one day, each one of us has thousands of such correlations as part of the basis upon which to ground our generalizations. So I'm inclined to think that Norman Malcolm's criticism, though interesting, is less than compelling.

To the extent that Thomas Reid's analogical thesis seems to require a private language, it faces all of the difficulties that Wittgenstein brought to bear on the very notion of a private language—after all, that was the old beetle-in-a-box objection. But this criticism, too, fails to reach Reid's position—which, as it happens, is very close to Wittgenstein's own. The language Reid is referring to is a natural language, not the artificial language of aches and pains. Indeed, Reid's natural language matches up quite well with what Wittgenstein called *natural expressions.*

We might say that both Reid and Wittgenstein are establishing the criteria according to which the judgments we make about the interior life of another are warranted. Certain natural expressions satisfy the relevant criteria and constitute a warrant for believing that someone else is happy, or in pain, or is angry. It's not that they say, "I am in pain;" it's that their behavior matches up in the right way with the behavior we are engaged in when we have that sensation.

It should be clear that our recognition of other minds constitutes the basis of one of the most important ingredients of social life, which is empathy. Our conduct toward others and what we expect from them both depend to a very considerable extent on our ability to project ourselves into their situation, and vice versa. It is doubtful, however, that such an important foundation for relationships between and among living beings would be reserved solely to human beings. Some recent evidence suggests that mice are, of all things, empathic! I do wish that this interesting finding did not require the little creatures to be caged and pestered, but we can only attempt to solve one problem at a time.

Well, what about this one? Scientists at McGill University performed a series of experiments in which cage-mates were inflicted with one or another distressing or painful stimulation. For example, one of the mice had an abdominal injection of a weak acid, the effect being the repeated stretching and the extension of their hind legs. When a cage-mate was put into the same cage, lo and behold, the cage-mate—having been injected with nothing—displayed the same behavior. Moreover, when two injected mice were placed together inside a cylinder, they spent more time writhing than when they were injected alone. It is interesting that these effects took place only with pairs of mates who had lived together for at least a week.

Now, I would not presume to conclude that findings of this sort establish a similarity between human and nonhuman forms of empathy. Nor, however, do I regard the human form of any characteristic to be the last word on that characteristic. What it takes to make it through a troubled and troubling world is obviously different for a mouse and a man. Sometimes, in our enthusiasm for evolutionary ways of thinking, we tend to regard a dog as sort of unconsciously striving to become an ape, who, in time, and with comparably great effort, might become the mayor of San Diego. I jest, of course, but I do wish to make a serious point: Selection pressures operate quite differently on different species. Here again, it is a pragmatic standard that establishes what is likely to find its way into succeeding generations.

What I would be prepared to conclude from research and critical reflection, at least tentatively, is that nature fits us out—all of us, mice included—with certain basic tendencies and dispositions. We are thereby able to adjust to certain significant environmental conditions without having to learn how to cope with everything! Just how nature goes about establishing these tendencies and dispositions is to be settled by those at a much higher pay grade than my own.

Surely the easiest way to settle the problems that seem to be plaguing us is by simply refusing to grant any special status to consciousness at all. Let's see what happens once we insist that all that exists is just one or another kind of physical thing. This surely gets us out of the bind. All we have to do is embrace physicalism, which is our next port of call.

Lecture Seven
Physicalism Refined

Scope:

We have seen some of the difficulties associated with explaining mental events on the basis of physical evidence. In this lecture, we examine two alternative theories, the *identity* theory, which does not accept that there are uniquely mental events, and the *supervenience* theory, which requires that a person cannot move from one mental state to another without moving from one physical state to another.

Outline

I. Two alternative perspectives to explaining mental events on the basis of physical evidence are the *identity* theory and the *supervenience* theory.

　A. The counterintuitive character of the identity theory presents difficulties, while its particular strength lies in the fact that it does not aim to explain causal relationships between mental and physical events; it does not accept the proposition that there are, in fact, bona fide and uniquely mental events.

　　1. Although there are various forms of the identity theory, they all proceed from an ontological position according to which there is only one kind of entity in reality, namely, physical reality.

　　2. Thus, all forms of the identity theory adopt *monistic materialism* (or *monistic physicalism*), a term that pays deference to the fact that not everything physical has mass, for example, an electric charge.

　　3. Monistic physicalism asserts that whatever has real existence is physical.

　　4. Monistic physicalism explains immaterial entities with examples such as lightning, which is, in actuality, an electrical discharge.

　B. Philosophers use an identity of *reference* to distinguish from an identity of *meaning*.

　　1. The terms *Morning Star* and *Evening Star* refer to the same entity. Although two sentences containing these terms may well have different meanings, they have identical referents.

2. Similarly, it is not that electrical discharges cause lightning. Electrical discharges *are* the lightning; both terms refer to the same phenomenon.

C. The identity theory can be illustrated thus: When Samantha says she has a toothache, she is referring not to a mental state but to a brain state.

    1. One argument to this effect has been advanced by the philosopher J. J. C. Smart (b. 1920) who, because he regards it as unbelievable, rejects an ontology that requires two radically different forms of reality, one physical and the other—who knows what?

    2. The identity theory is parsimonious in that it reduces reality from a two-substance to a single-substance affair.

II. Is the identity theory sound?

A. In its usual form, the identity theory asserts that mental states and processes, properly understood, are actually states and processes taking place in the brain.

    1. On this account, there is actually only one set of states and processes, namely, neurophysiological states and processes, not *mental* states as such.

    2. The identity theory establishes the mental as physical.

    3. The identity theory asserts that there is not a relationship between two distinct entities, only one entity for which we seem to have two modes of expression.

    4. This can be summarized by saying that M is identical to P, where M = mental states and P = physical states.

B. Considering the soundness of the theory requires considering the nature of identity relations in general.

    1. The philosopher Gottfried von Leibniz (1646–1716) advanced a criterion for testing such alleged identities.

    2. Leibniz's criterion of the identity of the indiscernibles proposes that distinguishing the mental from the physical could be ascertained by substituting a statement about a given mental state with one about a specific brain state.

    3. For example, defenders of the identity thesis would say that there are not two ontologically distinct events to explain a toothache, one being pain and the other being neurophysiological events in the brain.

4. Applying Leibniz's criterion would show that the toothache pain is just a brain process—just one process.

5. But some have argued that there is something that might be truthfully said about pain that could never be truthfully applied to statements about brain processes without a fundamental alteration in the truth of the statement itself.

C. Other objections to the identity theory include the position that however mental states and physical states are to be understood, it surely is not the case that, if they are identical, they are so *necessarily*.

1. We can imagine a world in which there are mental events without there being any physical events or a world in which mental events and physical events simply occur in parallel.

2. Obviously, the identity thesis cannot plausibly maintain that mental events just are physical events and are so *necessarily*.

D. Defenders of the identity theory get around this difficulty by arguing that the identity in question is not one of necessity but one of *contingency*.

1. Of all the things that mental events conceivably might have been, it is just contingently the case that they are physical events.

2. That the specific person having a toothache is Samantha is said, here, to exemplify a *contingent identity*.

3. Yet Venus is itself, and necessarily itself, no matter how many distinct names (e.g., Morning Star and Evening Star) are assigned to it. That is a necessary truth, not a contingent fact.

4. We accept that, of all the names a baby might have been given, Samantha was the contingent choice, and thus, we agree that the woman with the toothache is contingently named Samantha. But we do not agree that, of all the women Samantha might have been, she is just contingently herself!

E. Saul Kripke (b. 1940) in his *Naming and Necessity*, published in 1980, distinguished between what he termed *rigid designators* and *proper names*.

1. What Kripke argued is that objects picked out by proper names are never necessarily identical to any set of properties or conditions.
2. Rigid designators, on the other hand, are what they are *in all possible worlds*.
3. An entity is itself necessarily.
4. Therefore a particular mental state remains what it is in all possible worlds, whereas the brain states that would serve as candidate substitutes are not necessarily what they are in all possible worlds.

F. It is probable that every version of the identity theory will finally be jettisoned for several reasons.
   1. Suppose it is the case that there is nothing in the domain we call the "mental" that is anything but a collection of physical events and processes within the cranium and the balance of the body.
   2. Then, one conclusion to be drawn from the theory, if it is true, is that it is not consequential.

III. The theory of *supervenience* owes its currency to Donald Davidson's essay "Mental Events."

A. According to Davidson, mental characteristics have a relationship with physical characteristics that is dependent— or supervenient—on them.
   1. In its usual form, the theory does not begin by denying mental states.
   2. Defenders of supervenience theories are willing to retain the ordinary language used to refer to various states and properties associated with psychological life, as well as to refer to various common items, such as tables.
   3. In the case of a wooden table, for example, the wood supervenes on something more fundamental, namely, molecules, and the molecules supervene on atoms, and so on.
   4. We understand that there are not two ontologically distinct realms: one with a dining room table and another with atoms. We accept that the table is constituted of materials, some of them invisible, but absent these, there would be no table.

5. A table cannot change its shape without an alteration in the physical properties on which the visible and palpable property of shape supervenes.

6. In terms of mental states, two persons cannot be different in the pains that they feel without the underlying neurophysiological processes being different; a person cannot move from one mental state to another without moving from one physical state to another.

B. The problem with supervenience theory is that in every application of it where it seems sound, the properties in question do not match up with anything that makes the "mind-body problem" a problem.

Essential Reading:

Armstrong, D. M., *A Materialist Theory of the Mind.*

Kim, J. ed., *Supervenience and Mind: Selected Philosophical Essays.*

Poland, J., *Physicalism: The Philosophical Foundations.*

Questions to Consider:

1. If physicalism is true, what difference would it make?

2. If physicalism is true, what happens to the concept of personal responsibility?

Lecture Seven—Transcript
Physicalism Refined

So far in this series of lectures on consciousness, I've dealt with some of the difficulties associated with explaining mental events on the basis of physical evidence. In this lecture, I want to examine two alternative perspectives referred to respectively as the *identity thesis* and *supervenience.* At first blush, both are likely to seem quite strange as theories, especially the first. I'll begin with that one: the identity theory.

It has been advanced in various forms by a number of different philosophers; and, as I will attempt to show, it does face hardships unique to itself, not the least of which is its counter-intuitive character. Its particular strength lies in the fact that it doesn't set out to explain causal relationships between mental and physical events. Indeed, it doesn't deal with causality at all, for it doesn't accept the proposition that there are, in fact, bona fide and uniquely mental events.

Although there are various forms of the identity thesis, they all have this in common: they all proceed from the same ontological position, according to which there is only one kind of entity in reality, and that is a physical entity. We can say, then, that all versions of the identity thesis adopt *monistic materialism.*

From time to time, it is useful to qualify this very expression, by referring instead to monistic physicalism. This is really little more than a refinement, based on the fact that not everything physical has mass, as such. There are physical entities, such as charge, which are not material. So, as I say, the more precise designation is that of monistic physicalism, which asserts that whatever has real existence is, finally, physical. I note, however, that *physicalism* and *materialism* are generally regarded as interchangeable, and I might use them in just that way.

Now, what about thoughts, hopes, desires, and feelings? Are we to assume that these are nonexistent? For most of us, it would be far easier to assume that there is no physical reality than to assume that there are no thoughts, hopes, desires, feelings, etc. How could we even agree to accept the identity thesis itself, except on the assumption that we are capable of—what?—knowledge and belief.

Well, the defense of the identity thesis begins not with a denial of knowledge or belief, but with an example of how such terms are to be understood. Let's take as an example that of lightning. Most of us have had the experience of bright flashes across the sky, accompanied by thunder. "Look," we say, "it is lightning!" Now, our remote ancestors also saw the sky light up this way. In all ages that provide a record of meteorological events, there is evidence of lightning. But what is lightning?

Well, as it happens, the phenomenon we call lightning is an electrical discharge. This was true long before we had a theory of electricity. It was true long before anyone knew about electrical discharges. If we were to say even to the most intelligent of the ancient Greek scientists, "What you are calling lightning in your language is actually an electrical discharge," presumably he would have no idea what we were talking about. Of course, we do get the English word *electricity* from the ancient Greek root, *electron*; but this is obviously beside the point.

Now, let's take another example. Over the ages, people have become quite familiar with identical twins. The world's languages have phrases that identify such twins as being identical. The basis upon which the judgment is made is the striking similarity in appearance, and the simultaneous time of birth for the two twins. However, in a surprisingly large number of instances in the past, fraternal twins have often been incorrectly identified as identical.

Modern technology makes this misidentification more or less impossible now, because we can actually compare the DNA samples from the two twins. Let's ignore this and simply recognize that what we mean by the term *identical twins* has meant the same thing, over the long eons of human life, and long before anyone knew anything about DNA.

There surely were times when the accepted explanation for the appearance of identical twins was based on theories about the gods. Presumably, the goddess presiding over births had the power to create identical twins. Now, a people holding this belief surely had words for the presumed divine power that results in identical twins. We can make up a word; we can call it *toos-a-like*.

Toos-a-like, we see, turns out to be very much like *lightning*. Just as we accept that there is lightning, we accept that there are identical twins. What the identity theorist wants to make clear, however, is that in these instances, there is not both *toos-a-like* and DNA. Rather, the fundamental answer to the question, "By what means were identical twins brought about?" is "Identical DNA."

Now, similarly, there is not something properly called *lightning,* in addition to there being electrical discharges. Rather, if the word *lightning* refers to anything, it refers to electrical discharges.

What we have here are examples of what philosophers call an *identity of reference*, which is distinguishable from an *identity of meaning.* When we refer to the Morning Star and the Evening Star, we often mean different things. Among other considerations, one of these words refers to the time of observation. The time of day when persons would call Venus the Morning Star is quite different from the time during which we use the name Evening Star.

Now, if someone were to take up lodgings in the house of an astronomer, and were to ask, "What time is breakfast served?" only to be told, "As soon as you can see the Morning Star," the guests would surely know that breakfast will be served well before noon. But note that there are not two stars, even though for centuries even the most scientifically advanced people did not know that Morning Star and Evening Star—Phosphorous and Hesperus—were two terms referring to—what?—a single object. Thus, the terms Morning Star and Evening Star exemplify an identity of reference, though the terms do mean different things in different contexts.

Now, what about the lightning? If I were to say that, "On cloudy days, featuring loud thunder, it is very likely that there will be electrical discharges taking place in the sky," I might be saying something that is somewhat different in meaning from, "On a day like today, there's likely to be lightning." Clearly, however, what is referred to in those two sentences is the same phenomenon. It's not that the electrical discharges *cause* lightning; it's just that in such instances, electrical discharges *are* the lightning.

Now, with this much clear, we can illustrate the identity thesis this way: When Eleanor says she has a toothache, she is referring not to a mental state, but to a brain state. A proper understanding of the toothache is not that it is causally brought about by an event in the brain, but that it just *is* an event or process in the brain.

One very influential argument to this effect was advanced by the Australian philosopher J. J. C. Smart, in an article titled, "Sensations and brain processes." The article is nearly fifty years old, but it retains its freshness, and expresses a position as current within philosophy of mind as anything said more recently. I want you to listen to these lines from Professor Smart's early essay of about a half century ago:

> There does seem to be, so far as science is concerned, nothing in the world but increasingly complex arrangements of physical constituents. All except for one place: in consciousness. That is, for a full description of what is going on in a man, you would have to mention not only the physical processes in his tissues, glands, nervous system, and so forth, but also his states of consciousness: his visual, auditory, and tactual sensations, his aches and pains. That these should be *correlated* with brain processes does not help, for to say…they are *correlated* is to say that they are something "over and above." You cannot correlate something with itself. You correlate footprints with burglars, but not Bill Sikes the burglar with Bill Sikes the burglar. So sensations, states of consciousness, do seem to be the one sort of thing left outside the physicalist picture, and for various reasons I just cannot believe that this can be so. That everything should be explicable in terms of physics…except the occurrence of sensations seems to me to be frankly unbelievable.

Well, Smart's thinking here was an extension of earlier arguments along the same lines by Professor U. T. Place, and also by Herbert Feigl; both moved by the same commitment to ontological economy, similar to Smart's commitment.

What Smart rejects—because he regards it as (to use his word) "unbelievable"—is an ontology that requires two radically different forms of reality, one physical and the other—who knows what?

Well, there is no doubt but that the identity theory is parsimonious. It reduces reality from a two-substance to a single-substance affair and puts no strain on the credulity of the physicalist.

Pleased to have this parsimony, we then face, nonetheless, two insistent questions: Yes, but is it true? And, in any case, at what price do we gain this parsimony? After all, the desire for parsimony is surely worth a good bit, but not the family fortune! It may sound exotic by contemporary standards, but philosophy really is something of a search for truth; and, to the extent that it is, we have to know more about a theory than the economies it might produce. We also want to know if it is sound. And to make this determination, we have to be sure that we're clear on just what it is the theory asserts.

In its usual form, the identity theory declares that mental states and processes, properly understood, are actually states and processes taking place in the brain. On this account, there is actually only one set of states and processes, namely, neurophysiological states and processes. There are not mental states as such, enjoying some reality of their own, apart from the physical reality that includes everything else. Thus, if we persist in our use of mentalistic terms, it can only be for reasons of habit, or convenience, or for that matter, sheer ignorance. The more informed we become, so the argument goes, and the more willing we are to abandon old habits, the more the language of the physical sciences will replace such mentalistic terms. Even if we choose to retain the mentalistic language, we will do so with the certain knowledge that it refers to physical processes and events.

We see, then, that the identity theory establishes the mental as the physical; that there is not a relationship between two distinct entities, but only one entity, for which we seem to have two modes of expression. We might summarize the theory by calling any and every so-called mental event M and any and every physical event P. The identity theory can now be compressed as, M is P. If, in fact, our words for sensations, thoughts, feelings, and so forth, actually refer to anything; then what they refer to is something physical, namely, some physical event or process in the brain.

Well, to ask if a theory of this sort is true, or at least logically coherent, requires us to consider the nature of identity relations in general. Where such identities are alleged, there is a traditional test of sorts that must be passed; a test advanced by the philosopher Gottfried von Leibniz. It's often referred to as Leibniz's criterion of identity. Leibniz's criterion of the identity of indiscernibles, as the phrase has it.

A somewhat technical way of expressing the test is this: *A* and *B* are identical, just in case everything that can be truthfully said of *A* can be substituted as a statement about *B*, without there being any alteration in truth value of the statement. Implicit in this is that the things we say about *A* and *B* are relevant in the metaphysical sense. Mental states and brain states differ, of course, in the sense that the word "mental" has six letters, whereas "brain" has only five letters.

Obviously, this difference is not at all metaphysically relevant to the issue. Instead, the test of the identity of the mental and the physical would be in this form: Whatever might be truthfully said about a given mental state can be substituted by a statement about a specific brain state, without there being an alteration in the truth value of that statement.

Well, perhaps it's time to apply the test. Let's choose as a mental state Samantha's nasty toothache. We note that Samantha is in pain. Now, as noted, a fair amount is known about the neurophysiological correlates of pain. We know about the unmyelinated c-fibers whose activity leads to further events taking place in specific regions of the brain. Defenders of the identity thesis would want to say, in this circumstance, that we do not have two ontologically distinct events to explain; one being Samantha's pain and the other being events taking place in Samantha's brain. There is, in fact, just one reality here—Samantha's brain process. Samantha's pain just *is* this brain process. Now, if this is so, then, by Leibniz's test, there should be nothing truthfully and relevantly said about Samantha's pain that could not be substituted as a statement about Samantha's brain processes.

Some have argued, however, that there actually is something that might be truthfully said about Samantha's pain that could never possibly be truthfully applied to statements about Samantha's brain—or, for that matter, about any physical event or process. When Samantha says that she has a toothache—assuming here that Samantha is not attempting to deceive us—well, what Samantha says, goes! Reports that she gives about her pains are said to be incorrigible. There isn't some device external to and independent of Samantha that she must consult in order to learn if she is correct in declaring that she has a pain. We say that she enjoys a certain epistemic authority or epistemic privilege when it comes to her own pains, or at least statements about her own pains.

It would be quite peculiar for her to say something like, "If I'm not mistaken, I'm in intense pain." But, of course, it would never be peculiar for Samantha to say something like, "Unless I am mistaken, I am in brain state X." Samantha can't be mistaken about being in intense pain, but she surely can be mistaken about anything she might say about her own brain states, or anyone else's brain states, or any physical event or state at all.

We see, then, that there seems to be a class of statements—statements about one's own sensations—that cannot be substituted as statements about physical things, without there being some fundamental alteration in the truth value of the statement itself. We might say in this case that Leibniz's law of the identity of indiscernibles has been violated. I note here, but only in passing, that if there is an exception to Leibniz's law, it might be found in the field of quantum physics; but such exceptions would not seem to vindicate the identity theory as applied to physicalism. All sorts of odd possibilities arise within the context of quantum physics, and some of these will be reserved to a later lecture in this series.

I should say there are other objections to the identity thesis to which philosophers have given greater or lesser weight. We take the proposition that a thing is itself as necessarily true. Ontologically, that the Morning Star is the Evening Star is a necessary truth, in just the sense that one thing cannot be two things.

However mental states and physical states are to be understood, it surely isn't the case that if they are identical, they are so necessarily. That a thing is itself is true in all possible worlds. But we certainly can imagine a world in which there are mental events without there being any physical events, as well as a world in which mental events are causally brought about by physical events, or a world in which mental events and physical events simply occur in parallel. Obviously, the identity thesis cannot plausibly maintain that mental events just are physical events and are so necessarily.

Well, to get around this difficulty, defenders of the thesis have argued that the identity in question is not one of necessity, but one of contingency. On this account, it would go like this: of all the things that mental events conceivably might have been, it's just contingently the case that they turn out to be physical events. That is to say, of all the names the baby might have been given, it's just the case that the name "Samantha" was chosen. That the specific person we've referred to as having a toothache is Samantha is said on this account simply to exemplify a contingent identity.

Well, there is much to be said for and against this particular gambit. My own metaphysical biases being what they are, I must admit to considerable skepticism regarding the very notion of a contingent identity.

Of course, there are many statements in which two terms have a different sense but refer to the same thing: witness "Morning Star" and "Evening Star." As it required some deep thought and careful observation to discover that these two designations both refer to the planet Venus, we see that the identity amounts to an empirical discovery. The identity thus discovered was not that which obtains between what are essentially synonyms of the sort, "Bachelors are unmarried men." Nonetheless, that Venus is itself—and necessarily is itself, no matter how many distinct names are assigned to it—is not a contingent fact, but a necessary truth. We accept that, of all the names the baby might have been given, "Samantha" was, let's say, merely the contingent choice. In that case, we can agree that the woman with the toothache just is contingently named "Samantha." But we surely do not agree that, of all the women Samantha might have been, she is just contingently herself.

There is much more here, some of it a bit thorny, that really should be consulted. Renewed interest in the very logic of identities was ushered in by Saul Kripke in a very famous book titled *Naming and Necessity,* which was published in 1980. Kripke distinguished between what he termed *rigid designators* and *proper names.*

Consider the proper name "Napoleon." On the two sides of an alleged identity relation, we place "Napoleon" and "Lost the decisive Battle of Waterloo in 1815." Now, clearly, of all the military officers who might have lost that battle, we can say it's not logically necessary that Napoleon happened to be that officer. There are other conceivable worlds in which France wins this war of 1812 or where Napoleon never enters military service. Well, without belaboring the point, what Kripke argued is that objects picked out by proper names are never necessarily identical to any set of properties or conditions. Rigid designators, on the other hand, are what they are in all possible worlds. Napoleon remains himself if he exists at all, and an entity is itself necessarily.

Now, what has this to do with the identity thesis? Well, let's return to Samantha's pain. It is quite clear that there may well be a possible world in which discharge patterns from unmyelinated c-fibers result in the sensation of sweetness. In point of fact, it is surely plausible to think that any number of animal species endure something akin to pain, including species that do not have c-fibers. However, it is not plausible to think that in some other possible world, pain is not pain. So here again, we do not have an identity of indiscernibles, as Leibniz might have put it. We have a particular mental state that remains what it is in all possible worlds; whereas the brain states that would serve as candidate substitutes are not necessarily what *they* are in all possible worlds.

One or another form of identity theory is alive and well within philosophy of mind—and I surely would not suggest for a moment that the criticisms against it have been fatal. A faithful tool in all of philosophy is the educated hunch, and my own educated hunch is that every version of the identity theory will finally be jettisoned, and for several reasons, not all of them logically compelling.

Suppose it is the case that there is nothing in the domain we are pleased to call the *mental* that is anything but a collection—no matter how complex or elusive—of physical events and processes taking place somewhere within the cranium—and, let's say, the balance of the body. The emphasis here is on nothing. In other words, everything that is thinkable, everything that is felt or desired, everything that is known—all this and more finally turns out to be no more than expressions of our physicality. Fine! In that case, nothing whatever changes. Thought, desire, feeling, social interactions, and civic life—all of the problems and possibilities of life as it is actually lived—remain exactly what they are; for by the very terms of the alleged identity, they must be so.

It would seem that one conclusion to be drawn from the theory is that, if it's true, it's not really at all consequential! One has every right to expect of a revolutionary theory that it will change things. But all this theory does is burden us with a language, which we are not used to using, as if we would thereby understand more completely things that are fairly well understood with the language we have long used. Well, to say no more, that's not an especially appealing theory.

Is there another gambit, one that saves the language but spares us the housekeeping duties created by a two-substance ontology? Might supervenience do the trick? Now, as commonly employed in philosophy of mind, the term *supervenience* owes its currency to Donald Davidson's seminal essay, "Mental Events." Davidson summarized the thesis this way:

> Mental characteristics are in some sense dependent, or supervenient, on physical characteristics. Such supervenience might be taken to mean that there cannot be two events exactly alike in all physical respects but differing in some mental respects, or that an object cannot alter in some mental respects without altering in some physical respects.

It is an uncommon word, but one that expresses any number of ordinary facts. That structure we call a house *supervenes* on bricks and the mortar used to build it.

In its usual form, the theory of supervenience does not begin by denying mental states. Rather, defenders of the theory are willing to retain the ordinary language used to refer to various states, all the properties associated with psychological life.

They're also willing to retain the ordinary language used to refer to various common items, such as houses and tables. Consider the dining room table. We say it's a long rectangular table made of maple. No doubt but the dining room contains a table. However, every property that qualifies it as a table we now see supervenes on something more fundamental; in this case, on maple wood. Of course, the wood supervenes on something more fundamental, molecules; and the molecules on atoms; and the atoms on subatomic particles, etc. If we accept all this, we understand that there are not two ontologically distinct realms, one with dining room tables and another with subatomic particles. Rather, we accept that the table as given in experience is constituted of materials, some of them invisible; but, absent these, there would be no table.

Taking our more prosaic example of a table, we might say that a table cannot change in its shape or density or color, without there being an alteration in the physical properties on which these visible and palpable properties supervene.

Well, now let's get back to the issue of mental states. We see that what the supervenience thesis requires is this: two persons can't be different in the pains they feel without the underlying neurophysiological processes being different. A person can't move from one mental state to another without moving from one physical state to another.

There's much to recommend in this theory, but it seems to me the problem with it is that, in every application where it seems sound, the properties in question just don't match up with anything that makes the mind–body problem a problem. It's obviously the case that a wooden table is not only made of wood, but that wood it is a composite of elemental physical materials; but I don't know that anyone ever seriously contended that a table was anything else.

Well, what about mental events and thoughts? What about qualia— the very nature of the experience itself? Can this be explained on the basis of supervenience? We shall see.

Lecture Eight
Consciousness and Physics

Scope:

It has been argued that the real problem with physicalism is that we do not know enough about matter itself. The explanation of the phenomenon of mental life may demand a physical science beyond our current reach. In this lecture, we look at arguments from the laws of thermodynamics and quantum physics in pursuit of a solution to the question of the unification of the physical and the mental.

Outline

I.   Radical versions of physicalism fail at the level of our intuitions.

    A. We rely on intuitions, where neither the force of logic nor the evidence of sense supports one account at the expense of all other accounts of complex phenomena.

    B. Thoughts are not like things, and feelings have no shape, which is sufficient for most persons to view the physicalist agenda as excessively optimistic.

    C. More than one philosopher has suggested that such a judgment is premature.

        1. Galen Strawson (b. 1952), in his book *Mental Reality*, argues that the real problem with physicalism is that we simply do not know enough about matter itself.

        2. On an agnostic materialism view, the perplexing nature of the mind-body problem stems from unreasonable faith in our understanding of the fundamental nature of matter.

        3. Strawson remains committed to monistic physicalism, but he remains neutral, or as he puts it "agnostic," as to just what the physics of it all will prove to be.

        4. It is important to keep in mind that physics at the micro level is still a fairly young subject.

II. There are reasons to doubt that our current understanding of physics is up to the task of explaining conscious life, while the possibility remains that physics—especially quantum physics—may yet be able to do so.

A. The Oxford mathematician and theorist Roger Penrose (b. 1931) sets limits on the extent to which contemporary physical science may be viewed as promising in relation to the problem of consciousness.

B. Penrose concludes that the phenomenon of mental life may require a physical science not yet at hand.

   1. Kurt Gödel developed a mathematical theorem known as the *incompleteness theorem*, which holds that a mathematical system of sufficient complexity to include an arithmetic is logically incomplete; arguments external to it must be imported in order to render it complete.

   2. In light of Gödel's theorem, Penrose concludes that the proper model of human cognition is not computational, for, if the essential nature of human thought were computational, the limitations imposed by Gödel's incompleteness theorem would be manifest.

   3. We are able to reflect on our own problem-solving maneuvers without importing into the system some set of axioms, otherwise unknown to us, in order for us to make sense of what we are thinking.

   4. To say that we do not need such an external problem-solving apparatus is to say, among other things, that the essential character of human consciousness is *non-algorithmic*.

   5. Penrose concludes that mental life is simply not explicable in terms that physics now offers us.

C. Many think that the physics we have at least rules out alternatives to physicalism, if we consider the first and second laws of thermodynamics.

   1. The first law establishes that the internal energy of a system is equal to the heat added to the system minus the work done by the system.

   2. To insist that the term *energy* is reserved solely to physical forms is simply to assert physicalism, not to establish its adequacy; there could be some sort of *mental* energy. The first law of thermodynamics is neutral as regards the form of energy.

   3. The second law asserts that in any closed system, if anything physical is brought about, it is at the cost of energy in the system.

4. Another conception of the law is expressed in terms of *entropy*; unaided by external influences, entropy (or "disorder") tends to increase. To oppose this, work must be done and must be supplied from sources external to the system.

5. From this, we can see what troubles the physicalist about the idea that mental events bring about bodily events. To have such an effect, the mental events would have to supply energy, and this would be a measurable property of the system.

D. The thermodynamics argument is less than convincing.
   1. In purely formal terms, the thermodynamics equations are neutral as regards the nature of the units on each side of the equal sign.
   2. Furthermore, thermodynamics laws apply to closed systems in a state of thermodynamic equilibrium, and defenders of mental causation can argue that at least some psycho-physical transactions find the system neither closed nor isolated.
   3. In the real world, systems are permeable to all sorts of external influences, giving ample opportunity for anti-entropic outcomes.
   4. It is sometimes argued that evolution itself violates the entropy version of the thermodynamic laws, for, through evolution, there is a progressive increase in complexity and organization.

III. The prospect has been raised that consciousness and quantum physics are in some bizarre way interdependent.

A. One of the most influential schools of quantum physics, the so-called *Copenhagen school*, has argued that the results of experiments at the micro level can be understood only in terms of the influence of the act of observation itself.
   1. Niels Bohr's model of the atom restricts the locations that electrons can occupy when moving from one orbital plane to another; they are entirely probabilistic, as are the energy-level transitions themselves.
   2. Further theoretical developments, driven by experimental results, present a microcosm in which the particles occupy multiple states and multiple locations at the same time. The very act of measurement "collapses"

these to a single state, namely, a now specifiable single location and state.

3. David Bohm (1917–1992) furthered the speculations of Eugene Wigner (1902–1995) on the connection between quantum physics and consciousness, applying the theoretical and observational aspects of quantum physics directly to the functions of the brain and to the problem of consciousness.

4. Bohm, with his student Yakir Aharanov, showed that an electromagnetic field could have effects in spatial regions otherwise fully shielded (the so-called *Aharanov-Bohm effect*, which violates the core canons of classical physics).

5. Bohm later advanced the thesis that the brain at the micro (quantum) level is an informational system such that the mental and the material merge.

B. Suppose the Copenhagen interpretation is correct, namely, that it actually is the case that only by way of observation and measurement, by way of the introduction of some element or derived product of consciousness, that quantum uncertainties "collapse" into determinate states.

1. The influence that consciousness or its derivatives might have is not by way of contact but by way of that dimensionless entity, information.

2. The very nature of consciousness remains still unaddressed.

C. The essence of quantum phenomena is statistical.

1. What quantum physics overturned, at least at the level of micro- physics, is the classical world of absolute space, absolute mass, and absolute motion.

2. The essence of normal, adult mental life, however, is the capacity for logical modes of analysis and argument; modes of comprehending the broad divide that separates all that is "probable" from that which is necessary.

3. The world of quantum physics is a world of pure contingency, while the world of formal logic is one of pure certainty.

4. There appears to be some sort of "modal" mismatch between the probabilistic nature of quantum reality and

the necessities attaching to the conscious construction of such abstractions as mathematics and logic.

5. Quantum effects, owing to their statistical nature, become more accessible at the level of observation in the form of averages arising from innumerably large events at the level of particles.

6. The brain possesses billions of neurons and comparably innumerable connections among them. At any given time, we might consider the functioning brain as the averaged outcome of all these small activities.

Essential Reading:

Albert, D., *Quantum Mechanics and Experience*.

Bohm, D., and B. J. Hiley, *The Undivided Universe*, chapter 15.

Lockwood, M., *Mind, Brain, and the Quantum: The Compound 'I'*.

Supplementary Reading:

Heisenberg, W., *Physics and Philosophy*.

Questions to Consider:

1. Quantum events are inherently probabilistic. Are they a good model for mental events?

2. If reality is finally a composite of mindless quanta, how could I "know"?

Lecture Eight—Transcript
Consciousness and Physics

Radical versions of physicalism fail at the level of our intuitions. I don't mean to suggest by this that our intuitions are the last word on what can be accepted as true or false. But we do rely on these intuitions where neither the force of logic nor the evidence of sense supports one account at the expense of all other accounts of complex phenomena. Thoughts are not like things, and feelings have no shape. This is sufficient for most persons, even keeping an open mind, to regard the physicalist agenda as excessively optimistic, if not grandiose.

That such a judgment might be premature has been suggested by more than one philosopher. Galen Strawson, in his book, *Mental Reality,* argues the real problem with physicalism is that we simply don't know enough about matter itself. He calls himself an *agnostic materialist,* and he puts his position this way:

> According to agnostic materialism, the idea that the mind–body problem is particularly perplexing flows from our unjustified and relatively modern faith that we have an adequate grasp of the fundamental nature of matter at some crucial general level of understanding, even if we are still uncertain about many details.

Galen Strawson remains committed to monistic physicalism; but he must remain neutral or, as he would have it, agnostic, as to just what the physics of it all might in the future turn out to be.

I regard this as a properly modest position to take. Although the age of Newton—not to mention achievements in the ancient world—have supplied us with detailed knowledge of the physical world at the macro level, it is important to keep in mind that, at the micro level, at the level of particles, the science of physics is a fairly young subject. It is not only young but, by historic standards, entirely surprising. I'm not sure how physicists prior to 1900 would have reacted to the fact that, for example, the neutral B meson goes from its particle to its antiparticle state at a rate of some three trillion times each second. They never faced such a challenge, in part, because the measurement of events occurring at such a rate was simply impossible. And what might they have said about there being six flavors of quarks, not to mention a strange quark, into the bargain?

In all, then, the expectation that physics will provide an increasingly detailed and, perhaps, ever more surprising account of the material world is sound and sensible. It would also seem safe to conclude, even at this early date, that if consciousness ever proves to be something finally and ultimately physical, it surely will not be that at the macro level of chunks of brain tissue, but at the level of subparticles.

Accordingly, if the physicalist is to press on with attempts to ground consciousness in physics, there is good reason to believe that it would be quantum physics that would have to do the job. I will return to this later in this lecture, but I want to consider first some reasons for doubting that our current understanding of physics is up to the task of explaining conscious life. The future will speak for itself.

I must be cautious here, for the easiest way to don the fool's cap is to declare as impossible what science, often in a matter of decades or even years, shows to be nothing less than inevitable! When we modestly suggest that a particular and only quasi-scientific perspective on an issue may prove *always* to be insufficient, we must make clear that our position is based on some sort of conceptual analysis, and not on the facts and methods of science as such.

The distinguished Oxford mathematician and theorist Roger Penrose may be said to have put the ball in play with two extremely interesting books: the first titled *The Emperor's New Mind*, which appeared in 1989; and the second, *Shadows of the Mind*, which appeared in 1994. Both of these works seek to set limits on the extent to which contemporary physical science may be viewed as promising in relation to the problem of consciousness. The works are not at all pessimistic, but they are realistic. As with Galen Strawson's view that we don't know enough about matter itself, Penrose's position—based on an exacting analysis of physics and its mathematical foundations—reaches the conclusion that the phenomena of mental life may require a physical science—an entire physical science—not yet at hand. The issues here are complex, in some instances far too intricate to be covered in a general lecture. Perhaps I can convey at least the main points leading Penrose to the conclusion he has reached.

We might best begin with a proof in mathematics known as the *incompleteness theorem*, and advanced by Kurt Gödel. He published his landmark contribution to mathematics in 1931 in an article titled, "On Formally Undecidable Propositions." The generalization arising from his analysis can be expressed this way: Any mathematical system

©2007 The Teaching Company.

of sufficient complexity to include an arithmetic, will be based on axioms and theories that cannot be proven within the system itself. In other words, the system is logically incomplete. Arguments external to it must be imported in, in order to render it complete.

Now, in light of Gödel's theorem, Penrose concludes that the proper model of human cognition could not be computational, for if the essential nature of human thought were computational, the limitations imposed by Gödel's incompleteness theorem would be manifest. Well, this was manifestly not the case with Gödel himself; nor is it the case with the rest of us once we have Gödel's theorem explained.

Clearly, and by way of our own conscious life, we are able to reflect on our own problem-solving maneuvers without importing into *our* system some set of axioms, otherwise unknown to us, in order for us to make sense of what we are thinking. To say that we do not need such an external problem-solving apparatus is to say, among other things, that the essential character of human consciousness is (technical term here) *non-algorithmic*. Taking the term *algorithm* as referring to a set of problem-solving axioms, we conclude that our own conscious achievements are, as I say, non-algorithmic.

Is human thought the only form of non-algorithmic process? Not at all. But if we search through the vast realms of the physical, what we turn up by way of other non-algorithmic processes are just those that are described as random. Now, whatever we might want to say about our own conscious resources, we surely are not so modest—may I say, not so crazy—as to regard them as random. Were it otherwise, there couldn't be a Roger Penrose or, for that matter, an audience able to comprehend his work. Let's put all this together: Penrose reaches the conclusion that mental life is simply not explicable in terms made available by the physics now on offer.

But might the physics we have at least rule out alternatives to physicalism itself? Many think so, and they defend the judgment by invoking the first and second laws of thermodynamics. The party is getting rough, as you can see.

The first law expresses the conservation of energy, establishing the equivalence of heat and work. Stated briefly, the first law establishes that, the internal energy of a system is equal to the heat added to the system minus the work done by the system. If we express this as an equation, the statement is $\Delta U = Q + W,$ where ΔU is the change in the internal energy of the system, Q is the heat added to the system, and W is the work done by the system.

Of course, to insist that the term for and the concept of energy is reserved solely to energy in its physical form is simply to assert physicalism, not to establish its adequacy. It would be a form of question begging. When we say that one side of the equation for the first law of thermodynamics contains energy, we are not required to commit ourselves as to the nature of the energy in question.

Perhaps I might be permitted to invoke the notion of psychic energy— gads!—hopeful that this would not commit me to the care of a psychiatrist. Well, let's just agree that there may be—that there *could* be—some sort of energy of a type that would vindicate dualism or mentalism. Its very nature is such that our devices for detecting and measuring physical energy will never be affected by this form of energy. Nonetheless, let's say it does enter into the equation for the first law of thermodynamics; let's call it M for mental energy. Well, we now might modify the First Law to say that $\varDelta M + \varDelta U = Q + W + M$.

To the added heat in the system, we've added some mental energy on the left side of the equation; and, when all is said and done, the system has used all this to do some kind of physical work *(W)* and, yes, some mental work *(M)*. We can all be content that the equation works; the first law of thermodynamics is obeyed. We should be happy. Is all this weird? Yes! Is it ruled out by the law itself? No. Everything balances on each side of the equal sign; the law is honored. As I noted, the law can be entirely neutral as regards the form of energy, though legislative in requiring energy if work is to be done.

Well, now what about the second law of thermodynamics? What the second law asserts is that, in any closed system, if anything physical is brought about, it is at the cost of energy in the system. James Clerk Maxwell, in his *Theory of Heat,* summarized the second law this way:

> It is impossible in a system enclosed in an envelope which permits neither change of volume nor passage of heat, and in which both the temperature and pressure are everywhere the same, to produce any inequality of temperature or of pressure without the expenditure of work.

We see, however, that our modification of the first law will work here, too. There is still another conception of the second law, here expressed in terms of entropy—some know the second law best in the language of entropy. In this version, the law requires a constant increase in the entropy of closed systems.

How might we conveniently picture entropy? The distinguished physicist Richard Feynman, who was able, it seems, to see the world of abstract theoretical physics as if it were a collection of visible objects right in front of him, offered this way of understanding entropy: Imagine a closed system made up of a large number of tiny cubicles, each of them able to hold a molecule of gas. Let's say that we have been able to introduce gas molecules into that volume, and that the gas molecules are either black or white, but in equal number. Consider now the ways these might be arranged. In his *Lectures on Physics*, Feynman then brings the example to its informing conclusion. He says:

> If we have black and white molecules, how many ways could we distribute them among the volume of elements so that white is on one side and black is on the other? On the other hand, how many ways could we distribute them with no restriction on which goes where? Clearly, there are many more ways to arrange them in the latter case. We measure "disorder" by the number of ways that the insides can be arranged, so that from the outside it looks the same. *The logarithm of that number of ways is the entropy.* The number of ways in the separated case is less, so the entropy is less, or the "disorder" is less.

Unaided by external influences, the molecules will distribute themselves randomly; thus, the entropy will tend to increase. Now, to oppose this, work must be done, and it must be supplied from sources external to the system. Well, we begin to see what troubles physicalists about the idea that mental events bring about bodily events. To have such an effect, the mental events would have to supply energy, and this would be a measurable property of the system. How many mental ergs or joules are required to raise an arm?

Needless to say, if the argument from thermodynamics were that straightforward, the case for physicalism would be essentially won, for the only plausible alternative to it would then be seen as simply impossible. Well, matters are seldom this simple. The thermodynamics argument is less than convincing for several reasons. First, in purely formal terms, as I've indicated, the thermodynamics equations are absolutely neutral as regards the nature of the units on each side of the equal sign. All the law requires is that the sums come out right, whatever the chosen units prove to be.

Well, let's just suppose that there *is* some form of purely mental energy causally associated with bodily movements. Let's call the units of this energy *mentons*. The thermodynamics laws do not rule out mentons; they merely require that, at the end of the event in question, all the mentons can be accounted for. If the thermodynamics laws are obeyed, there cannot be a greater number of mentons after the work is done than there were before these mentons acted. That none of them will activate a voltmeter has nothing to do with it. Opponents of physicalism have already concluded that the world of volts, joules, and ergs is not the total world, for the total world includes something like mentons.

It should be recalled also that the thermodynamics laws apply to closed systems in a state of thermodynamic equilibrium. Well, defenders of mental causation can argue that at least some psycho-physical transactions find the system neither closed nor isolated, and that, in any case, the real world is rather less tame than all of this would imply. Once we come to grips with the lives of actual creatures in the real world, the model of a closed, isolated system in thermal equilibrium would seem hopelessly innocent.

The Nobel Prize-winning chemist Ilya Prigogine has drawn attention to this gap between the real, big, wide, and various world and the idealization of that world achieved at the level of theory. In the real world, systems are permeable to all sorts of external influences, such that there is ample opportunity for anti-entropic outcomes; outcomes in which disorganization is opposed by forces of organization; outcomes best described in terms of increased complexity and increased stability. Now, granted, this is surely a form of special pleading, but then so is the physicalist's promise that at some future time, when more is known about matter, physicalism will be vindicated. That, too, is a form of special pleading.

It is sometimes suggested that evolution itself violates at least the entropy version of the thermodynamics laws, for through evolution there is a progressive increase in complexity and organization. At the level of the individual organism, the same seems to apply in that, over the course of a lifetime, at least the larger creatures—including ourselves—acquire information, become more coordinated in their activities, more stable and settled in their lives, less random in their activities.

There is an enchanting if somewhat gothic picture of all this, in which we find ourselves on a narrow bridge between an earlier universe of mindless and maximum entropy and some ultimate universe just as mindless, just as maximally entropic. But here we stand, growing in knowledge and order, thereby making our own tiny little contributions to the overall forces that might, at least for a time, hold things together. I say this is an enchanting picture; the daily headlines offer a different picture, alas.

Well, I'd better stop with this before I lapse into punditry. But let me get to something even more daring: the prospect of consciousness and quantum physics being in some unexpected way interdependent.

From the earliest days of quantum physics, one of its most influential schools—the so-called Copenhagen school—argued that the results of experiments at the level of particle physics can only be understood in terms of the influence of the act of observation itself. The names most closely associated with this interpretation, notwithstanding to the contrary their disagreements with each other, are Niels Bohr and Werner Heisenberg.

Bohr's model of the atom replaced the tidy picture of a large nucleus with nice, round electrons revolving around it, as if this were a miniature solar system. Instead, the Bohr atom restricts the locations that electrons can occupy when moving from one orbital plane to another. Indeed, their positions are entirely probabilistic, as are the energy-level transitions themselves.

Even this model proved to be too stable to account for the growing number of experimental findings contradicting it. Further theoretical developments, driven by experimental results, present a microcosm in which the particles occupy multiple states and multiple locations at the same time. The very act of measurement, now, collapses these to a single state, which is to say, a now specifiable single location and state brought about by measurement.

Soon, and based on these considerations, quantum physics and consciousness began to form an odd couple in the learned discourse of the thinking classes. Eugene Wigner, one of the truly dominant figures of 20th century physics, speculated soberly on this connection between consciousness and quantum physics. The American-born physicist, David Bohm, who died in 1992, who had been an associate of Einstein's at Princeton, pressed on with Wigner-type speculations and applied the theoretical and observational aspects of quantum physics directly to functions of the brain and to the problem of consciousness.

I should say that David Bohm's is not a uniformly happy story, for he was caught up in the McCarthy hearings of the 1950s. His refusal to testify on 5th Amendment grounds led ultimately to the termination of his Princeton appointment and his subsequent emigration to Brazil, where he came to chair the physics department at Sao Paolo.

Well, let me do stay a moment longer with Bohm's line of reasoning, if not his politics. His unusual gifts as a physicist became widely recognized when, with his student Yakir Aharanov, he showed that an electromagnetic field could have effects in otherwise fully shielded regions of space—this, the so-called Aharanov-Bohm Effect, which violates the core canons of classical physics. Their published paper in 1959 contains this tantalizing passage: "contrary to the conclusions of classical mechanics, there exist effects of potentials on charged particles, even in the region where all the fields (and therefore the forces on the particles) vanish."

Bohm later pulled together the theory and mathematics of the hologram, and advanced the thesis that the brain, at the micro level— at the quantum level—is an informational system such that the mental and material merge. In an interview later published in 1986, he stated that matter and mind:

> ...are two aspects of one whole and no more separable than are form and content. Deep down the consciousness of mankind is one. This is a virtual certainty because even in the vacuum matter is one; and if we don't see this, it's because we are blinding ourselves to it.

Well, David Bohm was one of the few who could take on a problem as complex as that of unifying the physical and the mental. He wrote at length on the problem, one of the more accessible of his works being a book he wrote with David Peat titled *Science, Order, and Creativity*. It is no mark against his efforts to note that the efforts are purely conjectural and that, in a domain as rich in bramble and illusory paths as this one, speculators have things pretty much their own way.

Bohm himself, partly through the influence of his wife Saral, came to see quantum physics as also compatible with Buddhist thought; but here again, we can applaud the passion to know even while cautioning against tendencies toward the exotic.

I think the very achievements of modern physics have made all of us skeptical—toward what?—toward skepticism. Just as we had become comfortable with the orderly and mathematically framed world bequeathed by Newton and his contemporaries, well, along came the new physics and turned everything on its head. What more stable principle of logic than the impossibility of something *not* being itself; and then physicists give us the pairing of little matter–antimatter items whose states are simply indeterminable. The net effect of these revolutionary and unsettling discoveries has been to all but eliminate the expression, "But surely you are kidding!" As I say, then, we are far less confident in our skepticism than were our ancestors of the previous several centuries.

Well, would I be urging, then, the recovery of healthy skepticism? Of course I do. There is a great deal more to say about mind and matter, physics and consciousness; and unless all the theoreticians become Trappist monks, we can be sure that what needs to be said will be said.

Now, I don't enjoy membership in the august club of theoretical physics. I, as with many others, can do little more than peek through the windows and hope to catch a glimpse of what's being fashioned therein. One must be mindful, however, of the natural tendency to impute special powers of discernment to those who seem to understand fully what one scarcely comprehends at all. It's as natural as taking seriously what a great athlete or some admired actress might have to say about foreign policy or the space program.

Suppose the Copenhagen interpretation is correct; suppose it actually is the case that only by way of observation and measurement—by way of the introduction of some element or derived product of consciousness—that quantum uncertainties collapse into determinate states. It's quite obvious that the conscious element in all of this could be supplied from persons walking on the moon as by those making measurements of quantum states taking place in a laboratory in Switzerland. In other words, the influence that consciousness or its derivatives might have is not by way of contact, but by way of that dimensionless entity, information. It would seem that, even granting all this—even adopting the Penrose model of just how mental states result in the collapse of the wave front, or some such—we've come no closer to solving the problem of consciousness than we were a century ago. Still unsettled—I am inclined to say, still unaddressed—is the very nature of consciousness, the uniqueness of its possessor, the relationship to more specific mental states and functions.

There's something else that I find, if not worrisome, then at least peculiar. The very essence of quantum phenomena is statistical. What quantum physics overturned, at least at the level of microphysics, is the classical world of absolute space, absolute mass, and absolute motion. The very essence of mental life, however, at least at the level of normal, adult human life, is the capacity for logical modes of analysis and argument; modes of analysis and argument capable of achieving logical certainty; capable, that is, of comprehending the broad divide that separates all that is merely probable from that which is logically necessary.

But, just in case the right model of brain function is finally to be developed within the framework of quantum physics, then the right model of brain function will be statistical from top to bottom. The relaxation of wave fronts won't help here, for the conscious comprehension of logical necessity simply will not match up with anything that is itself and intrinsically wholly probabilistic and contingent. The world of quantum physics is a world of pure contingency; the world of formal logic, one of pure necessity. Although I'd not be so bold as to suggest, let alone declare, that ne'er the twain shall meet, I note the modal mismatch—this mismatch between the probabilistic nature of quantum reality and the necessities attaching to the conscious construction of such abstractions as mathematics and logic.

To this I might add yet another perplexity, though there are surely dozens more that might be added. Quantum effects, owing to their statistical nature, become more accessible at the level of observation in the form of averages arising from innumerably large events at the level of particles. The brain, of course, possesses billions of neurons, comparably innumerable connections among them. At any given time, we might consider the functioning brain as the averaged outcome of all these small activities. But we are not the sole possessors of brains, and if some sort of averaging of large numbers of small effects is what is to get us to consciousness, it would seem that nearly any brain will do; for that matter, any bit of excitable tissue should do. I'd be inclined to say that anything complex enough to be alive would do. Is it all that odd, then, that when the Prince of Wales thought it advisable to speak to plants, he might have been up to something? I suspend my skepticism, for the moment.

Lecture Nine
Qualia and the "Mary" Problem

Scope:

This lecture pursues the problem of physicalism through the examination of qualia, as framed by the philosopher Frank Jackson's famous "Mary" problem. We find that having scientific knowledge of natural phenomena is the not the same as having experience of such phenomena. Likewise, qualia are not successfully explained by reference to functional states.

Outline

I. The problem of *qualia* was framed by the philosopher Frank Jackson (b. 1943).

    A. In Jackson's analogy, Mary is a scientist who is forced to investigate the world from a black-and-white room via a black-and-white television monitor.

        1. She knows all about the physics of light and colors.

        2. When she is released from her black-and-white world, she finds that her previous knowledge was incomplete, although she possessed all the necessary physical information.

    B. *Qualia* refer to qualities that enter into our experience of things; for example, roundness and redness stand as qualia.

    C. Jackson argued that if physicalism were adequate in all respects, then to know everything about the physics of the situation is to know everything.

        1. If Mary knows everything about the physics of light, then presumably she knows everything about light.

        2. But if she knows everything about light, how is it that on entering the world of color for the first time, she now knows something that heretofore she did not know?

        3. Jackson argued that there is a kind of knowledge delivered to us by way of our experience that cannot be delivered any other way.

    D. This is not a new challenge.

        1. Johann Wolfgang von Goethe (1749–1832) published his *Theory of Color* in 1810, in which he contended that

Newton's theory of light explains everything except what we actually see.

   2. For Goethe, no matter how complete our understanding of the physics of light might be, that understanding alone cannot predict or explain the actual experiences we have of light and vision.

II. Are qualia the same for two different persons, and is there any method by which we can answer such a question?

   A. We could set up an experiment to test whether two persons see the same color, but it would tell us nothing about what might be called the "inner experience" of each of these persons.

   B. There is no reason to assume that identical physiological responses in two different persons unfailingly yield identical experiences.

   C. Nonetheless, there is a general tendency to regard the brain's record as somehow more valid or revealing than the mere utterances of actual persons.

III. Regarding the "Mary" problem, other philosophers have raised critical questions.

   A. Daniel Dennett (b. 1942) proposed that Mary is either lacking in relevant knowledge or has not made proper use of it.

   1. Assuming that Mary really does know everything, Dennett argues, Mary would have to know how the deep structures of the brain respond to information from the peripheral sense organs such that these brain mechanisms give rise to qualia.

   2. Even if Mary knew everything about the relationship between color experience and the physiology of the nervous system, absent reported qualia by actual persons about their own experiences, there would be no basis upon which to make any sense out of whatever data scientists had extracted from the brain.

   B. We must keep in mind that the brain is constantly active, the visual system responding incessantly to events that reach the retina.

   1. If this is going to provide the basis upon which to judge what an individual is seeing, it will never be enough to know only the activity going on in the nervous system.

2. There will have to be some way of tying particular events in the nervous system to the qualia reported by each individual.
3. It will be the qualia reported by an individual that provide the relevant data if the events in the nervous system are to explain *anything* about the experience.
4. Accordingly, it will not be the brain sciences, or brain sciences alone, that will settle the "Mary" problem.

C. Perhaps Jackson missed a major point in setting up Mary in a color-impoverished environment.
1. As the philosopher Paul Churchland (b. 1942) noted, conditions such as this will prevent the normal development of those mechanisms responsible for the processing of color information.
2. In light of these deficits, Mary cannot be said to know everything about the effect of light, for part of what goes into "everything" includes processes she is lacking.
3. Jackson's initial thesis is based on the assumption that Mary's visual system is normal, which suggests Jackson was just missing a significant piece of scientific information.
4. Churchland's rejoinder includes the fact that relevant experiences are necessary for us to learn about color in any way at all.

D. We could modify the "Mary" problem and have Mary exposed to poison ivy, to which she is allergic.
1. Mary knows that those who are allergic to poison ivy develop a rash and an itch.
2. It is not clear, however, that although she knew everything about this allergy before suffering from it herself, the actual itchiness presented her with something she could have claimed to "know" before the fact.
3. A description of an experience is different from the experience itself.

E. Jackson's "Mary" problem fails to distinguish between knowing *that* and knowing *how*.
1. I can read a book on all that there is to know about riding a unicycle, but I still do not know how to ride a unicycle.

2. But does this distinction between knowing *how* and knowing *that* actually get to the heart of the issue?

IV. Given the complexity of the nervous system, it is tempting to believe that all that hardware is surely able to bring about qualia.

    A. The qualia problem, however, is related to, but different from, questions about the factors that seem to be necessary for their occurrence.

        1. Ned Block (b. 1942) proposed the "Chinese nation" thought experiment, the point of which is that qualia such as pain are not successfully explained by reference to functional states.

        2. Similarly, Gottfried Leibniz proposed a machine he called a "mill" that could think, feel, and perceive, but an examination of its works would just reveal parts, not anything that would explain perception.

        3. In 1974, Thomas Nagel (b. 1937) questioned what it is like to be an entity that has experiences of a certain kind; he argued, "An organism has conscious mental states if and only if there is something that it is to *be* that organism."

    B. Experiences have a transforming effect, different from the effects of knowledge.

V. The problem of consciousness comes to be a problem because of certain core assumptions about physicalism that we are strongly inclined to make.

    A. While we may not be able to accept the idea that physics is complete, we tend increasingly to accept the idea that problems at the level of fact can be settled scientifically, if they can be settled at all.

    B. Consciousness seems to be the one fact in which all other facts are located, and this could be a key to a fuller understanding of the problem.

        1. Our awareness of consciousness is likely be heightened by our ability to compare times when we lose consciousness (through sleep, illness, and so on) against times when we regain it.

        2. Nevertheless, the number of times we lose consciousness in sleep has not significantly deepened our understanding of consciousness.

Essential Reading:

Block, N., O. Flanagan, and G. Güzeldere, eds., *The Nature of Consciousness: Philosophical Debates.*

Jackson, F., "What Mary Didn't Know," *Journal of Philosophy* 83: 291–295.

Nagel, T., "What Is It Like to Be a Bat?" *Philosophical Review* 4: 435–450.

Supplementary Reading:

Carruthers, P., *Phenomenal Consciousness: A Naturalistic Theory.*

Kirk, R., *Raw Feeling: A Philosophical Account of the Essence of Consciousness.*

Questions to Consider:

1. Did Mary *really* learn something when she first saw colors?

2. How does the "Mary" problem relate to the problem of "other minds"?

Lecture Nine—Transcript
Qualia and the "Mary" Problem

The title of this lecture is "Qualia and the Mary Problem." The problem was framed some years ago by the philosopher Frank Jackson, and I shall take a passage from his published article on this very subject. He sets up the problem very well. So here's the way Frank Jackson begins it:

> Mary is a brilliant scientist who, for whatever reason, is forced to investigate the world from a black and white room *via* a black and white television monitor. She specializes in the neurophysiology of vision and acquires, let us suppose, all the physical information there is to obtain about what goes on when we see ripe tomatoes, or the sky, and use terms like "red," "blue," and so on. She discovers, for example, just which wavelength combinations from the sky stimulate the retina, and exactly how this produces *via* the central nervous system the contraction of the vocal chords, and the expulsion of air from the lungs that results in the uttering of the sentence "The sky is blue." (It can hardly be denied that it is in principle possible to obtain all this physical information from black and white television, otherwise the Open University would of necessity need to use color television.) What will happen when Mary is released from her black and white room or is given a color television monitor? Will she learn anything or not? It seems just obvious that she will learn something about the world and our visual experience of it. But then it is inescapable that her previous knowledge was incomplete. But she had all the physical information. [Therefore] there is more to have than that, and Physicalism is false.

So there you have the *Mary problem* set up by Frank Jackson. The problem presented here is that nasty one, at least from the perspective of the physicalist: the problem of *Qualia*. *Qualia* is the plural form of the Latin *quale*, and refers to qualities. More specifically it refers to the qualities that enter into our experience of things. On this account, an object that is round and red will have these two qualities, and we would say that roundness and redness stand as qualia.

What Frank Jackson was arguing for—a position, by the way, that he subsequently retreated from—is that, if physicalism were adequate in all respects, then to know everything about the physics of the situation, is to know everything. If, in fact, Mary knows everything about the physics of light, then presumably she knows everything about light. But if she knows everything about light, how is it that, on entering the world of color for the first time, she now knows something that heretofore she didn't know?

One might be tempted to reply that what Mary comes to know entering the world of color, she knows by way of experiences. It just happens that, having been reared in black and white environments, she had no relevant experience; and, therefore, learned through experience that objects—which she always knew in some sense had color—give rise to experiences about which she previously had no knowledge. Well, yes! And this is precisely the point that Frank Jackson was making. There is a kind of knowledge delivered to us by way of our experiences, which cannot be delivered to us in any other way. I should say that Jackson's article caused quite a stir. As recently as 2004, an entire book has been devoted to the Mary problem, with the fetching title, *There's Something about Mary.*

I should pause, however, and note that this challenge is not a new one. I might call attention here to a work published in 1810 by the celebrated German genius Johann Wolfgang von Goethe, whose dates are 1749–1832. The title of the work in German was *Zur Farbenlehre,* generally translated as *Theory of Color.* What Goethe is at pains to establish in this lengthy work is that the Newtonian theory of light explains everything except what we actually see. Now this is not the place to examine the strengths and weaknesses of Goethe's own theory, which, I should say, by contemporary standards is scarcely adequate and on some key points patently false. He does present a number of novel notions and even novel findings of a most interesting sort; for example, that color experiences can be produced by black-and-white objects presented in a certain way. But this is beside the point at issue.

Here, at the very beginning of the 19th century, we find Goethe preparing the world for what will come to be called the *Romantic Rebellion.* To summarize this complex development all too briefly, I should say that it was a rebellion not against science, but against what's sometimes called *scientism*; against what had become something of the religion of science, arrogantly absorbing into itself the full panoply of human interests, desires, and wisdom. It was clear to Goethe that science was in no position to make such claims, and that the aesthetic domain especially was immune to its methods and perspectives. Goethe, we would surmise, would see no problem in the Mary problem, for he had already made clear that, no matter how complete our understanding of the physics of light might be, that understanding alone could neither predict nor explain the actual experiences we have by way of light and vision.

Well, what are these qualia? Are they ever the same for two different persons? Do Jack and Jill see the same red? Do they hear the same melody? Is there really any method by which we could even begin to answer such questions? I should say, there are approaches within experimental psychology that set out to settle matters of this kind. I can't say that they've settled the matter, but the approaches themselves are interesting and reasonable.

We might take an example of the question of whether two persons see the same red, and seeing what psychology does with it. Now, assuming that both persons know how to use color names, we might set up an experiment in which we present each of these subjects with lights that vary in wavelength and see the frequency with which they assign red to a given range of wavelengths. There may be conceptual reservations about the conclusion reached; but at least at a commonsense level, we might be willing to accept that both persons see the same red when they assign the term *red* over precisely the same range of wavelengths.

It is obvious that this method tells us nothing about what might be called the inner experience of each. It's not an experiment designed to settle the question of just what qualia are experienced by two different persons. But as of now, this is about as good an experimental approach as the question admits of. The approach is far more convincing than would be a comparison of the responses of the brains or the nerves of two different persons, for there is no reason to assume that identical physiological responses in two different persons will unfailingly yield identical experiences. If we want to know what people see, the best approach is to ask them.

Nonetheless, there is a general tendency to regard the brain's record as somehow more valid or revealing than the mere utterances of actual persons with their eyes opened. Well, suppose we share this impatience with mere verbal reports and wish to look into the machinery of things in order to settle the question as to whether two persons experience the same *qualia*. This is the course of action that Daniel Dennett recommends for dealing with the Mary problem.

As Dennett understands Mary's dilemma, she is either lacking in relevant knowledge or has not made the proper use of it. Let's assume, as Frank Jackson set up the problem, that Mary really does know everything. In that case, argues Dennett, she would have to know how the deep structures of the brain respond to information from the peripheral sense organs, such that these brain mechanisms give rise to qualia.

But surely this won't work. To begin with, even as Mary knows everything, she certainly doesn't know how brain mechanisms give rise to qualia, for no one knows how brain mechanisms give rise to qualia! Let's say, however, that Mary's knowledge does include what we have learned over the past century about the relationship between color experience and the physiology of the nervous system. We suppose further that she has focused very sharply on what has been discovered regarding brain responses to color. Her knowledge will include information as to how scientists establish these relationships. She will have learned that the scientists had to consult actual persons, and had to have confidence in statements they made about their actual experiences. Without the reported qualia by such persons, there would have been no basis upon which to make any sense at all out of whatever data the scientists had extracted from the brain.

We must keep in mind that the brain is constantly active, the visual system responding incessantly to events that reach the retina. If this is going to provide the basis upon which to judge what Jack or Jill is seeing, it will never be enough to know only the activity going on in the nervous system. There will have to be some way of tying particular events in the nervous system to—what?—the qualia reported by Jack and Jill. That is to say, somewhere down the line, and not very far down the line, it will be the qualia that provide the relevant data if the events in the nervous system are to explain anything about experience at all. Accordingly, at least at this point, it will not be the brain sciences—or at least the brain sciences alone—that could possibly settle the Mary problem.

Perhaps Frank Jackson missed a major point in setting up the problem. Now, he has Mary raised in a visually impoverished environment, at least with respect to color. As noted by the philosopher Paul Churchland, conditions such as this will prevent the normal development of those very mechanisms responsible for the processing of color information. Churchland is certainly on solid scientific grounds in arguing that the adult Mary will be seriously lacking in relevant neurophysiological functions. In light of these deficits, Mary cannot be said to know everything about the effect of light, for part of what goes into knowing *everything* will include brain processes, which arguably, she is lacking.

Now, is this a decisive criticism of the conclusions Jackson initially drew from the Mary problem? Well, if there is a last word to be said on this, it surely will not come from me. I'm strongly inclined to think, however, that the Churchland rejoinder will not work any more successfully than does Daniel Dennett's. To say that early childhood visual deprivation will prevent Mary's visual system from developing normally is correct as far as it goes. But Jackson's initial thesis is predicated on the assumption that Mary's visual system is normal. At first blush, this suggests that Jackson was just missing a significant piece of scientific information. Churchland's rejoinder includes the fact that relevant experiences are necessary for us to learn about color in any way at all. We learned to call something blue by associating that word with experiences brought about by light of relatively short wavelength. Absent the relevant experiences, such a word has nothing to tie itself to.

Now, again, this is fine as far as it goes. But let us modify the Mary problem this way: We stipulate a person whose visual system is entirely normal, and whose environmental history has been rich and complete in all relevant respects. We shall refer to our subject now as Mary 2. We now present Mary 2 with a nicely wrapped package—a cube, one foot on each side. Now, there are two facts that enter into Mary's complete knowledge of what soon will be seen to be relevant: The first fact is that some persons have an allergic reaction to ivy of a certain kind; we call it poison ivy. The second fact is that Mary 2 is one of those persons. But at no time in the past has Mary 2 been exposed to poison ivy. She does know, however, that those who are allergic to it develop a rash and an itch that may take days to clear up.

We decide to be a bit nasty here, in order to complete the experiment. So we blindfold Mary 2, and ask her to reach into the box and take out a present. Oh, and by the way, there is a nice present in there also; but there's a bit of poison ivy as well, just a slight amount. The predicted fact comes about: Mary 2 develops a slight rash, which she proceeds to scratch, soon to find some relief from a bit of cortisone topically applied.

Now, is it not clear, that although Mary 2 knew everything there was to know about the relevant allergy, about the fact that she suffered from that allergy, and the fact that the allergic response would include a rash and itchiness; that nonetheless, the actual itchiness presented her with something she could not have claimed to know before the fact? So Paul Churchland's rejoinder, though more refined and interesting than Daniel Dennett's, stands on the same ground. Both of them really do really seem to ignore the central point: The description of an experience is different from the experience itself.

Alas, there may be another rejoinder available to the physicalist, such that Jackson's Mary problem is seen to be specious; specious in the sense that it fails to distinguish between knowing *that,* and knowing *how.* Mary knows everything about the physics of light, and that means that she knows everything *that* there is to know about the physics of light. I may read a book describing everything that has to be known by one who would ride a unicycle. The book might contain whole chapters on the special difficulty of maintaining one's balance on a unicycle. Presumably I could then give lectures on the subject. But no matter how great my proficiency in knowing *about* these things, I still do not know *how* to ride a unicycle. Considered in this light, Mary's problem is actually the problem of not knowing *how* to assign color names; or *how* to do things with color; or, generally, *how* to match her behavior properly to phenomena involving color.

But does this distinction between knowing *how* and knowing *that* actually get to the heart of the issue? We all know what it is like to have experiences of a given kind. And we all know the difference between having experiences of the given kind and, in some sense, knowing what experiences of a given kind include at the level of fact or data. When Mary enters the world of color, quite apart from the question of whether she knows how to deal with it, it is apparent that she will have an experience that was unforeseen by her during the years in which she developed a thorough knowledge of the physics of light. Well, call me stubborn, but I do not believe that the *knowing that/knowing how* distinction matters much here at all.

Let's get back to the nervous system. Given its complexity and the richness of its interconnections, it is tempting simply to believe that all that hardware is surely able to bring about qualia. The problem of qualia, however, is related to but different from questions about the factors that seem to be necessary for their occurrence.

Consider a thought experiment proposed several decades ago by Ned Block. (This is odd, and wonderfully so.) It's often referred to as the *Chinese nation experiment*—China chosen here because of its very large population. In Ned Block's experiment, each citizen of China (stay with this now) is equipped to function as an individual neuron. Each has access to a telephone; has a list of numbers to call; and, in general, is able to enter into a complex network of information-transmitting fellow citizens. Ned Block sets up the pattern of phone calls so that, in time, it mimics perfectly the signals generated in an individual's nervous system and associated with—what?—the sensation of pain.

Now, on the standard account, what the Chinese nation has achieved through the actions of the entire population is nothing short of pain, though no citizen of China at the time is actually in pain. The point Ned Block was attempting to drive home in this very graphic example is that qualia such as pain are not successfully explained merely by reference to functional states, no matter how complex. The Chinese nation might mimic all the functional states taking place in the nervous system of one who is in pain, but the states thus brought about do not yield pain qualia.

One is reminded here of a much older thought experiment propounded by Gottfried Leibniz toward the end of the 17th century. It appears in a treatise he titled *Monadology,* which was published in 1688, where he considers the unique nature of perceptual experience. Here's Leibniz on the subject:

> It must be confessed that perception and that which depends on it are inexplicable on mechanical grounds, that is to say, by means of figures and motions. And supposing there were a machine, so constructed as to think, feel, and have perception, it might be conceived as increased in size, while keeping the same proportions, so that one might go into it as into a mill. That being so, we should, on examining its interior, find only parts which work one upon another, and never anything by which to explain a perception.

We can enter the mill envisaged by Leibniz or we can watch the entire population of China making phone calls and, in neither case, will qualia be explicated. Conscious experience seems to be one of those problems that just won't go away. At the same time, conscious experience seems to ground nothing less than our defining and essential nature.

On this point, I turn to an even more famous article in philosophy than Frank Jackson's. In 1974, the philosopher Thomas Nagel published an article with the intriguing title, "What is it like to be a bat?" The question here is not related to what it's like to be able to hang upside down from a tree; or to be featured in Dracula movies; or to nest in attics. Instead, the question gets at what it's like to be an entity that has experiences of a certain kind. Nagel puts it this way:

> The fact that an organism has conscious experience *at all* means, basically, that there is something it is like to *be* that organism. There may be further implications about the form of the experience; there may even (though I doubt it) be implications about the behavior of the organism. But fundamentally an organism has conscious mental states if and only if there is something that it is to *be* that organism— something it is like *for* the organism.

The criterion of consciousness here is not merely being awake; it's having experiences. In some sense, no matter how primitive, it is to be aware—to know of other events external to oneself or arising within oneself. Now, if we combine the Mary problem in Frank Jackson's essay and the criteria set forth in Thomas Nagel's essay, we can say that once Mary enters the world of color, she is now different. What it is like to be Mary A is different from what it is like to be Mary B. Experiences have a transforming effect different from the effects of knowledge as such.

As I have indicated in previous lectures, the problem of consciousness—of which the Mary problem is a particularly vivid example—comes to be a problem because of certain core assumptions that we are strongly inclined to make. I refer, of course, to the core assumptions of physicalism. We all respect—we're all the beneficiaries of—the achievements in science, many of which depend directly on a perspective that just is the physicalistic perspective. We treat ourselves to measured pride in the fact that we are not burdened by the antique superstitions of an earlier ages. We treat ourselves to measured pride that we take facts where we find them, and don't look for ghostly or wraith-like entities behind these facts. We might shy away from the confident assertion that, in principle, physics is complete; but we feel increasingly at home with the modest assertion that problems at the level of fact are to be settled scientifically, if they can be settled at all.

Well, if there is anything at the level of fact, consciousness must be it; for it seems to be that one fact in which all other facts are located. And in this we might find a key, if not a solution, at least to a fuller understanding of the problem itself. It is, indeed, consciousness that is the framework within which all other facts are located. For us as knowing subjects, there is no factual domain external to this framework.

I hesitate to press on with this point, for fear of seeming to be a guru. I'm tempted to employ the overworked analogy of fish in water. Of all the things a fish might discover, water is surely not one of them. Well, we are, as it were, immersed in consciousness in just the sense in which fish are immersed in water. Carrying the analogy a little bit further, we might be willing to grant that fish could learn how to speak about water. They might even engage in philosophical disputes regarding the *problem of water.* Like Mary, they might even learn everything there is to know about water. I wonder, however, if, even under such conditions, they would know what water *is,* really. Would they know it is wet?

We think we have a special advantage here, in that, every night, we lose consciousness. There are other occasions, such as the period just before sleep, when consciousness is greatly weakened. And then, too, there are conditions such as those associated with illness or trauma, where consciousness becomes temporarily eliminated. Now, to the extent that one recovers from all of these conditions, and is restored to full consciousness, one actually is more like a fish that can live in and out of water, and make the relevant comparisons. The analogy here suggests that fish may have the ability to discover water only when removed from it; we can discover the nature of consciousness owing to the fact that we lose it daily. Well, perhaps.

I must not become tiresome with appeals to the mystery of it all. I say only that I know what it is like to go to sleep, and then to awaken. I have the experience several hundred times each year. Excluding naps, but including my infancy, I would say this is an experience I've had perhaps 20,000 times. Speaking personally, I'd have to admit to being a very slow learner—for my understanding of consciousness has not been significantly expanded or deepened as a function of the number of such experiences. So too with all of the reliably recurring qualia with which experiential life is filled. Each quale might finally be translated into some number of impulses in some neuron somewhere in the brain. One might even learn, reluctantly or otherwise, to abandon the language of qualia, and adopt that of neurophysiology.

But at the end of the day, a rose by any other name will smell as sweet, and even as we attempt to translate the language of qualia into the language of physics, the very heart of the qualia themselves is left outside. More to come.

Lecture Ten
Do Computers Play Chess?

Scope:

Whether a machine is capable of thinking is a question that evokes the problem of other minds and one that found responses in the work of Alan Turing and John Searle. The latter's "Chinese room" analogy seeks to refute the relevance of computational power to the question of consciousness and intelligent behavior. Ludwig Wittgenstein posited that games and rules are cultural artifacts. Playing a game by the rules is not the same as getting the gist of a rule.

Outline

I. In 1997, the world's greatest chess player, Garry Kasparov (b. 1963), was defeated in a chess match with an IBM computer named "Deep Blue."

   A. The IBM computer was capable of processing 200 million chess positions per second, while Kasparov could process three or four positions per second.

   B. Moreover, the computer, unlike Kasparov, was not subject to physical phenomena, such as emotion and stress.

   C. Since chess strikes many as the quintessential activity of an intelligent being, Deep Blue offers an example of a machine outsmarting a human being.

   D. Kasparov, like Deep Blue, was the beneficiary of very special circuitry, a very special brain.

   E. If Kasparov's brain qualified him as an intelligent being, why would we deny Deep Blue the same status?

II. To appreciate the burden of this question, we turn to Alan Turing's 1950 article entitled "Computing Machinery and Intelligence."

   A. Alan Turing (1912–1954) imagined an "imitation game" designed to show that a machine, properly programmed to answer questions, will be indistinguishable from an intelligent human being.

   B. With stunning prescience, Turing claimed that one day the notion of machines thinking would be commonly accepted.

C. Turing was contradicted in his own time by a Professor Jefferson who held that machines could not be considered to have intellectual qualities unless they could create from feelings and emotions.

D. Turing refers to this objection as "the argument from consciousness." We cannot impute intelligence to a machine unless it is conscious of its own achievements.

    1. Turing examines the outcome of taking this argument to its extreme, which is essentially the solipsist point of view.

    2. Turing seems to be tracking the "problem of other minds" from a commonsense position: When something behaves and judges as we do, we assume it does so with the same psychological resources we need to do the same.

    3. If it were necessary to have direct knowledge of the consciousness attending the actions, then we could vouch only for ourselves as having minds—the solipsist point of view.

    4. Turing's devices accomplish what they do in a manner that seems similar to our own accomplishments, namely, by following established procedures and providing correct answers.

E. In his "Chinese room" analogy, John Searle (b. 1932) critiques this perspective.

    1. Persons ignorant of the Chinese language participate in an experiment in which they follow written instructions on how to arrange Chinese ideograms in a sequence that makes no sense to them but can be read by those who understand Chinese.

    2. What Searle seeks to establish here is the manner in which a seemingly mental achievement is gained by a process in which there is no comprehension whatever; it mimics the functioning of computers.

    3. Searle's "Chinese room" analogy tries to show the irrelevance of computational power to the question of consciousness and intelligent behavior.

    4. To accept the "Chinese room" analogy as establishing this is to accept that, in principle, the achievements in the field of artificial intelligence would leave untouched all the interesting questions about consciousness and understanding.

F. Thomas Nagel's question, "What is it like to be a bat?" infers that to be like something is to be the subject of some experience.

    1. There is no basis on which to impute any of Kasparov's emotions, fatigue, and so on to Deep Blue.

    2. It is not solipsism to deny consciousness to matter as long as we grant it to those like ourselves.

    3. With all due respect to Alan Turing, whatever Deep Blue is doing, it is surely not thinking.

III. If Deep Blue is not thinking, is it playing a game? To answer this, we must establish just what it is that makes any activity a game.

A. Any attempt to provide an exhaustive definition of what is a game is doomed to failure.

B. Ludwig Wittgenstein argued that games are recognized for what they are only by certain persons and under certain conditions.

    1. A game might be understood as an activity that expresses certain cultural forms and norms.

    2. The difference between a street fight and a boxing match, for example, is recognized for what it is only by those understanding various conventions, instructed within a given culture, and having a developed conception of what constitutes a "match."

C. But games are not only cultural artifacts; they involve rules.

    1. There is a distinction between the actual physical constraints that guarantee a given course of action and following a rule.

    2. A restaurant's "no smoking" rule would still be violated if we lit a cigarette and let it burn without actually inhaling it.

D. Do computers follow the rules of chess?

    1. Those who follow rules get the gist of the rules.

    2. Following a rule is not a built-in causal connection but, rather, a conventional one.

3. A given rule will apply across a virtually limitless number of instances such that no one could find them all in advance.
4. Computers do not "get the gist" of the rules of chess. Deep Blue was programmed to have its chess pieces move according to the rules of chess.

Essential Reading:

Penrose, R., *The Emperor's New Mind: Concerning Computers, Minds, and the Laws of Physics.*

Searle, J. R., *The Rediscovery of the Mind.*

Supplementary Reading:

Turing, A. M., "Computing Machinery and Intelligence," *Mind* 49: 433–460.

Questions to Consider:

1. Must there be consciousness for there to be "play"?
2. What are the necessary features of an activity that qualify it as a "game"?
3. Well, *do* computers play chess?

Lecture Ten—Transcript
Do Computers Play Chess?

Between May 3 and May 11, 1997, much of the world was riveted to radios and television sets by a chess match between the world's greatest chess player, Garry Kasparov, and an IBM computer named Deep Blue. Kasparov had been victorious a year earlier, but now Deep Blue had the benefit of upgrades presided over by top Grandmasters. Before this rematch, Kasparov spoke confidently about the inability of a computer ever to defeat a world-class chess player.

Indeed, after Kasparov won the first game of the rematch, his estimation of the weakness of computers seemed to be vindicated. But there would be a total of six games, three of them ending in a draw, and Deep Blue winning two of the other three. It was after the second draw that Kasparov admitted he was beginning to feel fear. In the end, Deep Blue delivered a humiliating defeat in the final game. Kasparov refused offers for another rematch, and Deep Blue was retired by IBM. Years later, in 2003, Kasparov again agreed to a match, this time with a computer named Deep Junior, but he achieved no more than a tie.

Now, there's no question but that the approach to the game of chess by Kasparov—indeed by any human being—must be quite different from the approach programmed into Deep Blue. The computer in this match had the capacity to process 200 million chess positions per second. Estimates of Kasparov's abilities in this regard suggest that he was able to process perhaps three or four such positions per second. Deep Blue had stored thousands of games played by Grandmasters over a course of many years. These results could be accessed by the computer with lightning speed. At 2,800 pounds and equipped with 516 chess processors, Deep Blue had the capacity to assess 50 billion board positions every three minutes. Any human being would be under a severe handicap facing computational power of this magnitude. Nor is a computer subject to distraction, fatigue, stress, or emotion; though some were inclined to describe Deep Blue's performance in psychological terms.

Writing in the *New York Times,* the newspaper of record, the day after Kasparov's defeat, Robert McFadden seemed eager to give the machine a personality. He put it this way:

It would be wrong, of course, to imagine that [Deep Blue] …has no personality. Throughout its six-game match with Kasparov over the last 10 days—indeed, for most of its four-year existence—it has exhibited qualities of scrupulous care, unshakable calm and remarkable powers of concentration and endurance.

Well, apart from the question of the extent of fear, distraction, frustration, etc.—as these things might influence the outcome of the game—such factors surely make it clear that whatever the computer is doing is different from what a human chess player is doing. Is it different in the sense of being superior, or in the sense of being just different?

Now, a small pocket adding machine can outdo any human being in the speed and accuracy of arithmetic calculations. A power drill can drill holes faster. An automobile can move more quickly than a sprinter. All in all, then, it should come as no surprise that a machine outperforms a human being. This, after all, is why we make machines in the first place. So, viewed in this light, we might ask just what it was about the Deep Blue–Kasparov match that seemed so different, and so riveted the world's attention.

Well, unlike drilling holes or even putting numbers in our heads, playing chess strikes many as the quintessential activity of an intelligent being; and if that's the case, then Deep Blue offers an example of a machine outsmarting a human being. Well, if only to be argumentative, I would note that a roadmap is something of an intellectual achievement. It records a very large number of locations; it lays out the shortest path along which to get from one location to another. But we don't attribute intelligence to a roadmap, because we regard it as nothing more than the printed version of something human beings have done. It's surely not the roadmap that figured out the locations and the various routes.

No one, however, was the Deep Blue that figured out the millions of board positions evaluated in less than a second. The information available in Deep Blue was put there. The very circuitry with which this information could be processed and integrated was also designed by human beings, and for that express purpose. Now, considered in this light, Deep Blue is reminiscent of a chess-playing machine that made the rounds as early as the 18th century. It astonished all onlookers, until it was discovered that a chess-playing midget was inside!

Well, let us turn the tables here. Garry Kasparov was not born knowing all the chess moves that would come to make him a grandmaster. And he, too, is obviously the beneficiary of some very special circuitry. One might say that he's the beneficiary of a very special brain, giving him uncommon powers of memory and decision making. If these gifts qualify him as an intelligent being, why would we deny Deep Blue the same status?

In order to appreciate the burden of this question, let me discuss a path-breaking article published in 1950 by one of the fathers of artificial intelligence, Alan Turing. The title of the article was "Computing machinery and intelligence," and it appeared in the journal *Mind*. Here's how Turing sets up the question and proceeds to answer it:

> I propose to consider the question, "Can machines think?" …I shall replace the question by another, which is closely related to it and is expressed in relatively unambiguous words. The new form of the problem can be described in terms of a game, which we call the "imitation game." It is played with three people, a man (A), a woman (B), and an interrogator (C) who may be of either sex. The interrogator stays in a room apart in front the other two. The object of the game for the interrogator is to determine which of the other two is the man and which is the woman.

Having set up the imitation game in this fashion, Turing goes on to claim that, if in the end the interrogator is satisfied that he has been dealing with two human beings—all this based on answers to specific questions—then it should make no difference in the end if one of the respondents turns out to be a computing machine. A machine capable of deceiving the interrogator is accomplishing something that we would all assume required thinking. With stunning prescience, Turning makes this claim: "I believe that at the end of the century the use of words and general educated opinion will have altered so much that one will be able to speak of machines thinking without expecting to be contradicted."

Alan Turing not only would have expected Deep Blue to perform as it did, but he laid the very foundations for that very performance. Why not consider Deep Blue as a participant in Turing's imitation game? Think of each of Kasparov's moves as a question: "What do you plan to do next?" And think of each of Deep Blue's moves as an answer to that question. This is an approximation to Turing's imitation game, and in light of the machine's performance, are we not, "...able to speak of machines thinking without expecting to be contradicted?" As it happens, however, Turing was contradicted in his own time. He cites a passage from a Professor Jefferson designed to raise the gravest doubts about machines having any intellectual qualities whatever. According to Professor Jefferson:

> Not until a machine can write a sonnet or compose a concerto because of thoughts and emotions felt, and not by the chance fall of symbols, could we agree that machine equals brain—that is, not only write it but know that it had written it. No mechanism could feel (and not merely artificially signal, an easy contrivance) pleasure at its successes, grief when its valves fuse, be warmed by flattery, be made miserable by its mistakes, be charmed by sex, be angry or depressed when it cannot get what it wants.

Turing refers to this objection as "the argument from consciousness." We cannot impute intelligence to a machine unless it is conscious of its own achievements. But, says Turing:

> According to the most extreme form of this view the only way by which one could be sure that machine thinks is to be the machine and to feel oneself thinking. One could then describe these feelings to the world, but of course no one would be justified in taking any notice. Likewise according to this view the only way to know that a man thinks is to be that particular man. It is in fact the solipsist point of view.

We see here that Alan Turing is tracking the problem of *other minds* as we discussed it in an earlier lecture, and seems to be taking the common sense position: When something behaves and judges as we do, we assume it does so with the same psychological resources we need to do the same. If it were necessary to have direct knowledge of the consciousness attending the actions, then we'd only be able to vouch for ourselves as having minds. This, says Turing, just is the solipsist point of view.

Now, we've already seen Thomas Reid's solution to the problem of other minds. It's based on the fact that we live lives very similar to those lived by other entities who look like us, and act like us, and speak the way we do. The devices Alan Turing has in mind do not share these properties. What they do accomplish, however, in a manner that may seem similar to our own accomplishments, is to follow established procedures and provide correct answers.

Now, the philosopher John Searle, in his famous analogy called the *Chinese room,* offers a devastating critique of this entire perspective. There are many variations of the Chinese room, and I will content myself here with a brief one. We agree to participate in an experiment. We are given a sheet on which are written certain instructions. These have to do with the manner in which we are to arrange certain cards that we're given once we enter the room. We are told to place cards with certain characters on them to the left or right of cards with other characters on them.

Now, as it happens, the characters are Chinese ideograms. We have no knowledge of the Chinese language. Nonetheless, we follow the instructions, and we arrange cards in a sequence determined by these very instructions. The completed set makes absolutely no sense to us at all. However, to those who know the Chinese language, the sequence makes entire sense, and it can be read competently by anyone knowing the Chinese language.

Now, what Searle seeks to establish with examples of this kind, is the manner in which a seemingly mental achievement is gained by a process in which there is no comprehension whatever. The sheet of instructions tells us only how to move objects around. We have no idea of the meaning of this sequence, or even if there is a meaning. We are functioning the way a computer's compiler program might function. With great speed and immense capacity, Deep Blue, on this account, is arguably doing the same thing—which is to say, *nothing* akin to playing chess.

Now, there have been many rejoinders to Searle and his conclusions about the in-principle limitations of artificial intelligence as a model of human cognition. What Searle hoped to establish by way of the Chinese room was the irrelevance of computational power to the distinct question of consciousness and intelligent behavior. To accept the Chinese room as establishing this much is to accept that, in principle, the achievements in the field of artificial intelligence would leave untouched all the interesting questions about consciousness and understanding. I offer the Chinese Room, however, just to make clear that the success of Deep Blue is subject to more than one interpretation.

Now, we find further critical appraisals by way of Thomas Nagel's question cited in the earlier lecture, "What is it like to be a bat?" The point of the question is that, to be *like* something is to be the subject of some experience. It would make no sense, to be like a clump of mud. By the same token, it might be argued that it makes no sense to be like a printed circuit—or a million integrated printed circuits. What it is like to be a chess player is, among other considerations, to be in a state of focused attention, thinking of possible gambits. A 2,800-pound block of hardware, on this account, is not like being *anything,* especially a thinking thing. What is it like to be Deep Blue? Well, unless there's some shared experience, some overlap in the form of life lived by us and by Deep Blue, we are left to conclude that it's not like *anything* to be Deep Blue!

Kasparov came to know fear in the rematch with Deep Blue. Presumably, he also experienced frustration and fatigue; anxiety and elation; confusion and confidence. There's no basis upon which to impute any of this to Deep Blue. It is not solipsism to deny consciousness to matter, as long as we grant it to those who are like ourselves. If we ask, "What is it like to be Garry Kasparov?" we have answers, no matter how incomplete or subject to error. It's like being an entity that endures fatigue and worry; that takes pleasure in success; that feels uncertainty in the face of certain options. It's also like being an entity that thinks.

Now, we can carry this empathic process elsewhere, and realistically ask what it's like to be dog; or a cat; or, yes, a bat. But as the circumstances of life become radically different from our own, and as the perceptual and behavioral capacities take on a radically different character, we soon lose touch. We can't even guess what it's like to be a clam or an amoeba, even though we're inclined to think that whatever has any kind of experience is something that it is like to be. Again, however, it is not *like* anything to be a machine; and if this is so, then—with all due respect to Alan Turing—whatever Deep Blue is doing, it surely isn't *thinking.*

Well, if not thinking, just what is the computer doing? Is it actually playing a game? Now, before attempting to answer this question, it's necessary to establish just what it is that makes any activity a game. Consider these games: chess, basketball, football, marbles, hangman, water polo, solitaire, pin the tail on the donkey. Consider two children playing house, where one is pouring tea into miniature cups.

Now look, not all of these activities result in victory and defeat. Not all such activities result in scores or points. There are literally thousands of games, and none of them is an exact duplicate of any other. Any attempt, therefore, to provide an exhaustive definition of a game would be doomed to fail.

The philosopher Ludwig Wittgenstein recognized this, and he understood that it's in the nature of games that they are recognized for what they are only by certain persons and under certain conditions. To use his own way of phrasing the matter, I would say that an activity is recognized as a game only by those living at least roughly the same form of life. Now, there isn't some specific structural or physical feature of an activity, such that anyone capable of seeing that feature would understand that the activity is a game.

Take the game of solitaire, or patience, for example. One might actually go through an entire deck multiple times without actually completing the set. A person unfamiliar with card games, watching someone placing cards over each other repeatedly, seemingly without rhyme or reason, would have no basis upon which to assume that a game was being played at all.

Or consider the difference between a street fight and a boxing match. The latter is recognized for what it is only by those understanding various conventions, instructed within a given culture, and having a developed conception of what constitutes a match.

Understood in these terms, an activity qualifies as a game insofar as it expresses certain cultural forms and norms. Games are not only cultural artifacts, but are used as cultural artifacts only by those who comprehend the nature of the game. Think of an alien who has no comprehension of the game of chess, and he proceeds to use the chessboard as a placemat. Yet, the alien is using the chessboard, but not as a chessboard.

Suppose Deep Blue consistently moved the bishop vertically and horizontally. Suppose further that Deep Blue persistently moved the rook diagonally. We would not say that the computer was playing chess poorly, but that it wasn't playing chess at all. It's necessary that the rules of chess be followed if we can say chess is being played. And the matter of following a rule is actually quite complicated and, on a certain understanding, presupposes nothing less than a form of acculturation. The distinction I wish to make here is between the actual physical constraints that guarantee a given course of action, and following a rule.

Suppose we enter a restaurant and we see a sign on each table that reads, "No smoking." We proceed to find a cigarette and, without putting it to our lips, begin to burn its tobacco leaves with a match. Although smoke is emanating from the cigarette, we are not smoking. Of course, management will quickly draw our attention to the fact that we are violating the rule against smoking.

Suppose, instead, that the habitual smoker, knowing he would not be able to smoke inside the restaurant, were to deeply inhale smoke before entering the restaurant, and then, once inside, exhaling all at once. And suppose he continues this practice, a puff at a time. Each time leaving the restaurant in order to inhale, then returning into the dining room to exhale. At no time is he actually smoking in the dining room. But clearly, however, he's violating the rule.

Now, how does one come to know that one is violating a rule? The example of smoking should make it clear that just about any rule is subject to a very wide range of applications and interpretations. Moreover, a given rule, if it's to be understood and obeyed, will apply across a virtually limitless number of instances, such that no one could possibly have all of them in mind in advance. We walk to a door in a hotel and we see a sign that says, "Do not disturb." Consider the linguistic and cultural resources one must have in order to know the ways in which others might be disturbed.

In his *Philosophical Investigations,* Wittgenstein cuts a path toward a fuller comprehension of rule following when he says, "a person goes by a signpost only insofar as there exists a regular use of signposts, a custom."

We bring our automobile to a full stop when we approach a red octagonal sign at an intersection. During the time, from early morning to the dead of night, when we might approach such signs, their actual hue and brightness will vary greatly. Depending on our approach, the actual shape of the sign as projected on the surface of the retina will be anything but octagonal. The sign may be in disrepair; it might not be standing straight. It might actually be part of a billboard advertisement and, thus, not require us to stop.

Again, rule following is not a mechanical affair but a cultural expression, not unlike wearing a feathered headdress or putting numbers on a mailbox. The Jones family live at 200 Spruce Street, next to the Smith family, who are at 202 Spruce Street. An alien who understands these numbers to be quantities might wonder if there is an invisible house at 201, or if items intended for both families should be addressed to the sum 402.

Do computers play chess? Well, we might now ask, do computers follow the rules of chess? Recognizing that rule following is not as simple as we might initially have thought, we have reason to hesitate here. On a certain account, there must be a veritable culture of rule following.

What I mean by this, following Wittgenstein, is that rule following is not unlike dressing, dining, or gardening; it's something that one is born into. The number of ways the activity can be engaged in is largely without limit. No one would live long enough to learn each instance of the activity. In point of fact, it really isn't something learned at all, if by learning, we mean memorizing words in an instruction manual. After all, the instruction manual is going to contain phrases such as, "Do not smoke," "Do not disturb," or "Do not move the rook diagonally." In each of these cases, there are myriad ways in which the rule might be obeyed or violated. Those who follow the rules are those who get what? Those who get the gist of the rules.

At the same place in his *Philosophical Investigations*, Wittgenstein says:

> Let me ask this: what has the expression of a rule—say a signpost—got to do with my action? What sort of connexion is there here?—Well, perhaps this one: I have been trained to react to this sign in a particular way, and now I do so react to it.

No one enters the world disposed to come to a halt in the presence of an octagonal sign. And a baby given a chess piece is as likely to suck on it as to throw it out of the crib. Just what is the connection between a signpost and what one does? It certainly isn't causal. There isn't some built-in connection between the projection of octagonal forms on the retina and the resulting activation of muscles, such that one comes to a full stop. Rather, the nature of the connection is the same as that which has the disappointed batsman sit down after swinging three times without hitting the ball. It is not a causal connection, but a conventional one, and is thus comprehended if it is to be obeyed; it is comprehended at a cognitive level, at a cultural level.

Now, let me make this clearer. Suppose our alien is also addicted to smoking, but comes from a distant planet with a different system of signs and rules. On that distant planet, anytime one sees a word with the letters *s* and *k* it is obligatory to put out one's cigarette—this tied in with certain religious doctrines. The alien now enters one of our restaurants and sees the sign "No smoking" and immediately crushes his lit cigarette. He has, I think you will agree, not followed the "No smoking" rule; he has followed a different rule. Note that the same behavior might be elicited by a sign, but might be governed by entirely different comprehended meanings.

I would be strongly disinclined to think that computers get the gist of the rules of chess. I would be strongly disinclined to think that computers get the gist of any rule at all. My disinclination here is not that of the humanist whose sensibilities are offended by the very thought of machines being intelligent. Deep Blue was programmed in such a way as to have its chess pieces move according to the rules of chess. Those responsible for the programming are the rule followers. Among the things that it is like to be like them, following rules is one of them. Of course, this is also one of the things that it is like to be a chess player. Do computers play chess? Well, only if they try.

To this point we've considered normal conscious life. In the next lecture, I'll add to our difficulties by presenting certain significant departures from the norm, and noting the special and additional problems that these create. So, you see, things are always rather more complex than we might have thought in the first place.

Lecture Eleven
Autism, Obsession, and Compulsion

Scope:

Knowing what happens when the functions of consciousness are defective may help us learn more about the nature of consciousness. In order to adapt to any particular environment, a normal sensory system resorts to active or passive filtration. This does not happen in cases of autism and other neurotic disorders. Moreover, those with such disorders cannot come to know what it is to be like someone else through conscious awareness and the integrative achievements of the mind.

Outline

I. Psychologists refer to our ability to continue a conversation when background noise is very loud as the *cocktail party effect*, and this includes the ability to control what we listen to when different sets of sound are present at the same time.

  A. To be conscious is to be *aware of something*, and the process by which we are able to direct our awareness is *attention*.

  B. Under normal circumstances, there are two principal means by which events in the external world are denied access to consciousness; both involve filtering.

    1. One means is fixed and based on the operating characteristics of a particular sensory system.

    2. The second means by which events in the external world are barred from entry into conscious awareness is that of *active* filtering, sometimes called *selective* attention (the cocktail party effect being a good example).

    3. In the absence of such filtering, it would be impossible to adapt to any environment.

  C. The relationship between consciousness and awareness is direct, as is the relationship between awareness and attention.

  D. If we cannot get outside our own consciousness in order to study it—in the same way that fish are not likely to *discover* water, for it is the abiding condition of their lives—we might nevertheless learn more about the nature of consciousness by seeing what happens when its functions are defective.

II. There has been a surge in research in recent decades of childhood conditions that affect the functions of consciousness.

   A. Two such conditions fall in the category of autism spectrum disorders (ASD) and include autism proper and Asperger's syndrome.

      1. Asperger's syndrome is a mild form of autism disorder syndrome, and sufferers often have an elevated sensitivity to noise or loud sounds.

      2. Those who suffer from autism spectrum disorders also have symptoms that seem closely tied to the failure to direct and maintain conscious awareness.

      3. Such children are slower in learning to interpret what others think and feel.

   B. Another such disorder is attention deficit hyperactivity disorder (ADHD).

   C. There are now many skeptics who are inclined to think that quite normal behavioral problems are being classified as one or another of these abnormal conditions.

   D. What is common across cases of autism is the obsessional nature of the controlling thoughts; in this regard, autism and obsessional neuroses have much in common.

      1. Persons suffering obsessional disorders engage in repetitive behavior that is organized and, at a certain level, meaningful, but finally serves no purpose.

      2. These activities commonly include such obsessions as the repeated checking of doors, locks, lights, and so on; the repetitive washing of clothes; or the verbal repetition, sometimes for hours, of a single telephone number.

   E. The flattening of emotion, so common in autism, ties directly in with the diminished capacity for empathy.

      1. Where the Asperger syndrome generates auditory defensiveness, the autistic syndrome seems to generate emotional defensiveness.

      2. The field of consciousness narrows as a consequence, and once narrowed, the correctives of reality have no means of access.

    3. The French psychologist Pierre Janet (1859–1947) theorized that neurosis at its base is the narrowing of the field of consciousness.

    4. On this account, neurosis is a disorder at the level of information processing.

F. Another tragic case was that suffered by the classical musician Clive Waring, who lost portions of his brain associated with memory.

    1. Waring, while in all respects conscious, alert, and aware, was unable to retain any memory of events that had taken place as little as half a minute earlier.

    2. Waring's search for his own mind was moment to moment, with nothing enduring.

III. Conscious life and awareness are not restricted to information processing in the neutral sense of information.

A. We are able to integrate what we hear in the voice and see on the face of another with that provided by the balance of the context.

B. Owing to certain normal and natural dispositions, the result of this integration is in the form of empathy and sympathy; we come to know what it is like to be someone else.

    1. This is an achievement of conscious awareness and the integrative achievements of mind, one that makes possible an understanding of lives different from our own.

    2. Try to imagine the quality of life available to those unable to perform these integrations and reach states of awareness.

C. It is never, however, a simple task to uncover what it is like to be someone else.

    1. Few have done as much to alert us to this as Dr. Oliver Sacks (b. 1933), whose book *The Man Who Mistook His Wife for a Hat* is based on clinical investigations of patients suffering from right-hemisphere brain defects.

    2. One of those patients displayed the full range of autistic symptoms yet could draw with amazing accuracy and in a manner that revealed a comprehension of the feelings of others.

D. We all engage in behaviors that to some degree could be labeled autistic, compulsive, or obsessional, but that does not mean that we know what it is like to be autistic or neurotic.

E. There are many other clinical conditions that display aspects of conscious life and awareness otherwise obscured by normal life.

   1. These include dissociative disorders, which might involve large gaps in memory or the adoption of multiple personalities.

   2. Another version—depersonalization disorder—finds the patient seeing himself at a distance and reflecting on his own behavior as if he were a disinterested witness.

   3. These conditions are especially intriguing because the patients have consciousness and are aware.

   4. Then, too, there are many altered states of consciousness, some caused by the use and misuse of drugs and alcohol.

Essential Reading:

Sacks, O., *The Man Who Mistook His Wife for a Hat.*

Supplementary Reading:

Baron-Cohen, S. *Mindblindness: An Essay on Autism and Theory of Mind.*

Questions to Consider:

1. Autism is characterized by greatly "flattened" emotions. Are emotions a necessary aspect of *mental* life?

2. How would you reply to someone who said that computers have minds but are "autistic" at the level of interpersonal and emotional life?

Lecture Eleven—Transcript
Autism, Obsession, and Compulsion

We have all found ourselves in a noisy setting, at a party or in the theater; perhaps in a crowded bus; perhaps in a large sports arena. Nonetheless, and even when the background noise is very loud, we've been able to continue a conversation with one or two friends. Psychologists refer to this as *the cocktail party effect*. It manifests itself in different ways.

For example, we place headphones on a person, and present sound dichotically. The presentation is dichotic when information is delivered to each ear separately. Thus, we might present the left ear with a popular poem, and, at the same time, present the right ear with a reading from the Bible. Now, the normal observer is able to control which of these two channels of information will be listened to. This itself illustrates the selective nature of attention. An observer can simply choose which stream of information to attend to, hearing either the Bible, or the passage from the poem.

But now here's an extension of the research. Establishing that the listener is attending to, say, the Bible passage—and we establish this by asking factual questions about the passage after it has been listened to—we then test the listener on what was presented in the unattended channel.

Now, let's compare the results: The Bible passage is delivered to the left ear, a poetry selection to the right ear, with the listener instructed to attend to the left-ear information. If we then test the observer, by having him repeat or recall whatever was heard in the left ear, performance will be nearly as good as if nothing had been played into the other ear. In fact, the ability to control our attention is so great that, under these conditions, the observer may actually hear nothing delivered to the other ear. In some studies, observers attending carefully to information delivered to one ear were found to be unaware that the other ear received passages in several different languages.

Aware; unaware: When we search for words that capture the essence of consciousness, the most common synonym is *awareness*. To be conscious just *is* to be aware, and to be aware is to be aware of *something*. Now, the process by which we are able to direct our awareness is just what we mean by *attention*. We will sometimes hear on a public address announcement, "Please direct your attention." And we do; or at least we can. It is often but not always under our control. Sometimes we are the ones who allow events to enter consciousness; and of course, at other times, we have no choice in the matter.

Now, under normal circumstances, there are two principal means by which events in the external world can be denied access to consciousness. Both involve filtering. One means by which external events are filtered out is fixed, and it's based on the operating characteristics of a particular sensory system. For example, human auditory sensitivity permits us to hear sounds in the frequency range of approximately 20 to 20,000 cycles per second, or *hertz*. Our sensitivity is greatest in the region of 3,000 to 5,000 cycles per second. Now, as sounds fall far below or rise far above this range, ever greater intensities of sound will be required if we are to hear them.

Dogs, on the other hand, are responsive to frequencies in the range of 40,000 to 50,000; mice upwards of 90,000; the whale to frequencies in excess of 120,000. Dog whistles are sold, and they are designed, to emit sounds that might be irritating to a dog, though entirely inaudible to us. Above a certain frequency, sounds are simply filtered out; not in the manner of the cocktail party effect, but passively.

The same is the case in all sensory systems. In human vision, normal color vision finds us seeing colors where the wavelength of light varies between approximately 360 and 760 millimicrons—a millimicron is a millionth of a meter, or a nanometer. Wavelengths below 360 move in the direction of what we call *ultraviolet,* whereas those above 760 are in the direction of infrared. Now, the honeybee is quite sensitive to ultraviolet radiation, and we are blind to it. Here again, we have an example of a passive filtering system, which has nothing to do with attention.

Now, the second means by which events in the external world are barred from entry into conscious awareness is that of *active* filtering. The process is sometimes referred to as *selective attention,* a good illustration of which is the cocktail party effect. In the absence of such filtering, it would be impossible to adapt to any environment. In noting the difference between plants and animals, Aristotle took the position that the line that ultimately divides the two was established by—what?—sensation. To use the phrase now familiar to those who have listened to these lectures, we might have Aristotle put it this way: Having sensations is what it is like to be an animal.

But the very sensitivity of sensory systems is such that we and other animals would be simply overcome by a flood of sensations, were we not able to filter out much that impinges on us. Think of the dog for a moment, whose olfactory sensitivity is so extraordinary. It is estimated that the single epithelial cell in the nose of the dog will respond to the dissipation of one molecule of fatty acid! In a world filled with aromas, a dog could never find his food, unless most of that world of smells could get filtered out.

The relationship between consciousness and awareness is direct. The relationship between awareness and attention is direct. The processes associated with these are extremely complex, and depend on normal functioning and the normal course of development.

I noted in an earlier lecture that fish are not likely to discover water, for it is the abiding condition of their lives. I said that consciousness creates a similar problem for us. But if we cannot get outside our own consciousness in order to study it, we might nonetheless learn more about the nature of consciousness by seeing what happens when its functions are defective.

In recent decades, there's been a surge in research concerned with the childhood conditions that significantly affect what are finally some of the functions of consciousness. There are profound deficits in the capacity to attend to things, to focus one's mental energies on a particular task, to set realistic goals and carry through, step by step, to their completion. The conditions have much in common, but medical specialists regard them as distinct. Two of them fall in the category of Autism spectrum disorders, or ASD, and include autism proper; and Asperger's syndrome; and there are numerous variants of each of these.

Asperger's syndrome, at least at the level of description, is a mild form of the Autism disorder syndrome. Those suffering from this condition often have an elevated sensitivity to noise or loud sounds of any sort. They seem to work overtime to filter out such sounds. They display what's sometimes referred to as a kind of *auditory defensiveness*. Considerable variation is found, of course, but in some instances, the auditory defensiveness expresses itself in the form of filtering out voices. In other cases it might be something as subtle as the sound of an electric fan that will cause great upset.

Autism spectrum disorders are not readily explained in terms of parental failure or insufficiently supportive environments. Specialists are in agreement that the signs of such disorders are often apparent in the first year of life, often very early in the first year. The National Institutes of Health provide a brochure for parents with a checklist as to what to look for. Consider what NIH includes among these signs: The baby doesn't babble, point, or make meaningful gestures by one year of age; does not speak one word by 16 months or combine two words by two years; does not respond to his or her name and, after beginning to learn some language, seems to lose it all at once.

There are also symptoms that seem closely tied to the failure to direct and maintain conscious awareness. The child is not able to make and keep eye contact with another. The sensory and motor links needed to engage in play seem to be poorly formed and quickly lost. Instead of playing with a toy, the child might simply put them in a line; or attend to an insignificant part of the toy; or be compulsively drawn to one toy to the exclusion of all the rest. And through it all, there may be indifference—a seeming deafness—to the surrounding social world of other persons.

When the NIH document turns to the social dimensions of these disorders, a picture that is at once melancholy and distressing emerges, all the more poignant for its clinical objectivity. Listen to the NIH brochure:

> Children with ASD also are slower in learning to interpret what others are thinking and feeling. Subtle social cues, whether a smile, a wink, or a grimace, may have little meaning. To a child who misses these cues, "Come here" always means the same thing, whether the speaker is smiling and extending her arms for a hug, or frowning and planting her fists on her hips. Without the ability to interpret gestures and facial expressions, the social world may seem bewildering. To compound the problem, people with ASD have difficulty seeing things from another person's perspective. Most 5-year-olds understand that other people have different information, feelings, and goals than they have. A person with ASD may lack such understanding. This inability leaves them unable to predict or understand other people's actions.

157

The incidence of these conditions is not negligible. As many as three or four children per 1,000 will be found to suffer from one or another version. Moreover, the incidence is far higher in boys than in girls—four times higher. Heredity has been implicated, for the siblings of a child suffering from one of these disorders are 75 times more likely than average to have the same or similar disorder. In addition to autism and Asperger's syndrome, there is now a veritable epidemic of attention deficit hyperactivity disorders, ADHD, having some similarity to the autism syndromes, but also significant differences.

Now, if only because of the seemingly sudden increase in the number of children thus classified, there are now many skeptics inclined to think that what is of "epidemic" proportions is just the inclination to classify ordinary and quite normal behavioral problems under one or another of these headings. One need not be a skeptic in order to find troubling the large number of young boys and girls on powerful prescription medications, not without worrisome side effects.

I should say, speaking personally, that not too many years ago, a college friend of mine, visiting his grandson in California, made an anxious telephone call to me, asking for advice as to whether his grandson should be given Ritalin. Now, although I knew what the answer would be, I asked what the basis was on which the medication was being proposed. Well, "They think he has an attention deficit syndrome," was the answer.

With just a few more questions, I was able to establish that the boy had a favorite football team, that he could not be torn away from the television set on Sundays, when his team was playing. In other words, he was able to direct and sustain his attention for hours on end! This didn't sound like an attention *deficit*. However, that he did not direct and sustain his attention in the classroom seemed to be the principal cause of alarm. Well, I should say, on that basis, one can only guess as to the number of young boys who might be candidates for medication!

Again, I do not rank myself among skeptics in an area such as this. As in most matters of this kind, however, caution is the order of the day. Healthy skepticism is not to be discouraged; but, of course, anyone who has had exposure to children and even infants suffering from the more severe forms of these conditions quickly surrenders doubt to the weight of evidence.

A number of years ago, public broadcasting and the BBC collaborated on a nine-part series titled *The Mind*. Serving as a consultant to that series, I suggested that the first program be titled "The Search for Mind." And we included in that program two truly tragic cases. One featured a young man suffering from autism. The form it took was not unusual. His emotions were clearly quite flattened relative to what would be normal. He spoke in a monotone. There was no time during the long interview in which he smiled, though at no point would one conclude that he was at all sad or angry.

His days were full. He would get on his bicycle, and enter on a tour he had prepared for himself, in which towns were to be visited in their alphabetical order. It was essential that this order not be violated for, if he missed a town, if he went out of the order, he would have to begin the journey anew, repeating the sequence in its entirety. When asked to account for the order in which he visited the destinations, well, he said it was governed by the alphabet. In other words, he took it as obvious that the order of letters in the alphabet should govern the order of locations visited. This was not an idea he could be freed from. It had entered into his consciousness as if it were a form of infection. And this was an infection for which there seemed to be no cure.

When I say in the form of his autism we find something not unusual, I don't mean to suggest that large numbers of autistic persons engage in projects of just this kind; but, rather, what is common across such cases is the obsessional nature of the controlling thoughts. In this regard, autism and obsessional neuroses do have much in common. Persons suffering obsessional disorders engage in repetitive behavior which is organized, at a certain level meaningful, but behavior that finally serves no purpose. The actions in question would be normal if performed once or twice, but they interfere with important aspects of life owing to the obsessional rates of occurrence.

Now, common among these activities are the repeated checking of doors, locks, light switches, and electrical appliances; the repetitive washing of clothes, scrubbing of floors, cleaning of hands; an orderliness so strict that there are files of files! In the course of a day, the person may spend hours counting by sixes, repeating their own telephone number, hanging their clothes in the closet, removing them, re-hanging them, dozens of times. And often, for those suffering this form of neurosis combined with obsessional thoughts and compulsive behaviors. Obsessed with her guilt, we find Lady Macbeth proceeding to wash her hands repeatedly.

The flattening of the emotion so common in autism ties in directly with the diminished capacity for empathy. It's as if one has compartmentalized within one's awareness the sheer physical facts of the environment, now stripped of their larger meaning and of the importance that others might attach to them. Where the Asperger syndrome generates auditory defensiveness, the autistic syndrome seems to generate a kind of emotional defensiveness. The field of consciousness has been narrowed. There's enough room for one or just a few items, and it is on this constricted content that all of the resources of consciousness are focused. Consciousness now thus narrowed, the correctives in reality have no means of access.

A century ago, the leading French psychologist, Pierre Janet, theorized that neurosis at its base just *is* the narrowing of the field of consciousness. On this account, neurosis is a disorder at the level of information processing, as we might be inclined to put it today. Or, put another way, the filters are too sharply tuned, the bandwidth too narrow, for reality to enter into awareness.

The second case featured in *The Mind* series, promoted so many years ago, is even more tragic. The reluctant hero of this was a well-known classical musician, Clive Waring. Portions of his brain, chiefly the hippocampus, associated with memory had been destroyed by encephalitis, and the result was a profound form of amnesia. He was unable to retain in memory events taking place even as little as a minute earlier. He was in all respects conscious, alert, and aware. Consciousness and awareness, however—our powers—are only as good as the information they have to work on, and Clive Waring's awareness, possessed of no more than bits and pieces of disconnected experience, did not allow him to form so much as a lived day, so much as a lived hour. The search for his own mind—this pathetic search— was moment to moment, with nothing enduring.

Now, as I said at the beginning of this lecture, we learned something about conscious life by examining the consequences of having something go wrong with it. In the normal course of events, the phenomenon of the *cocktail party effect* is taken for granted. We benefit from the fact that we are able to focus our attention on what matters to us. In fact, we often become even peevish when the world intrudes upon what does matter for us, and calls upon us to redirect our attention away from something that we were interested in.

But think of the hazards we would face were we unable to have our awareness thus redirected at all—ever! Imagine if we couldn't be distracted by the approach of the saber-toothed tiger; or the shouts of those who've noticed the outbreak of a fire; or cries for help coming from the lakeshore. These exemplify the hazards actually faced by those who suffer from the conditions I've summarized in this lecture.

Conscious life and awareness are not restricted to information processing. In that neutral sense of information, we have to admit, there's much more than that involved. We hear in the voice of another, and see on the face of another, evidence of grief, or joy, or hopefulness. We are able to integrate this information with that provided by the balance of the context. Owing to certain normal and natural dispositions, the result of this integration is in the form of empathy and sympathy.

Again, following Thomas Nagel's useful phrase, we come to know *what it's like to be* someone else, in a manner of speaking. And this is an achievement of conscious awareness, and the integrative achievements of the mind. It's the achievement that grounds social and interpersonal life. It makes possible an understanding of lives different from our own. Again, try to imagine the quality of life available to those unable to perform these integrations and reach these states of awareness.

Now, there is a caution warranted here, however. It's never a simple task to uncover what it's *like to be* someone else. We may have their words, and we may watch them behave, but this is about as close as we're likely to get to their interior lives. If the behavior is impoverished; if the words seem to be lacking in affective elements; if the voice is flat and the face somewhat fixed; we may greatly and gravely underestimate what is taking place within that field of consciousness to which our own access is inevitably incomplete.

Few have done as much to alert us to this as Oliver Sacks, especially in that celebrated book of his of 1985, *The Man Who Mistook His Wife for a Hat*. The book is based on clinical investigations by Dr. Sacks of patients suffering from right hemisphere defects. One of those patients, José, displayed the full range of autistic symptoms. Accordingly, he was largely neglected by the medical staff and ignored even by members of his own family. But having given José a pad and pencil, Sachs was amazed at the accuracy of the drawings so quickly produced. What one found in the drawings one would not have found in José's conduct, let alone his speech, which was utterly inarticulate. José produced sketches clearly revealing a comprehension of the feelings of others, things of importance, objects with a very deep meaning.

I recall as a graduate student in neuropsychology hearing a visiting lecturer say that everyone in the audience was epileptic. As the speaker was famous, and as we knew sooner or later some sort of examination would determine whether we were listening carefully, I recorded these remarks in my notebook, but listened even more carefully to the main point the speaker was attempting to convey.

Nerve and muscle are excitable tissues. Their intended function is to be active. The brain is an extraordinary ensemble of excitable cells. In the normal case, the level of excitation is just what is required for us to accomplish the sorts of things on which survival and progress depend. Nonetheless, every brain has a threshold for seizures. Now, those of us who would resist being called epileptic, and who have never had a seizure, simply have never faced the conditions capable of generating seizure activity in our brains. But such conditions there are!

Well, recalling the shock value of the speaker's surprising diagnosis of his audience, I'm tempted to heighten the awareness of my own listeners today by claiming that, well, we are all autistic, compulsive, obsessional, etc. Unless we're in treatment, or significantly limited in our attempts to get through the challenges of the day, we surely can take comfort in the fact that the world has not yet found stimulating or oppressive conditions sufficient to reveal full-blown autism, compulsivity, and obsessional neuroses.

But who has never returned from a meeting, or a party, or a social gathering, without recalling some offensive remark or minor insult that might actually grate on one for hours, or even days? In the language of today's therapists, we would be told not to "obsess"! But we do. And we often ignore otherwise clear signs of distress in others. We fail to display the joy and appreciation that the kindness of others warrants. We often continue to engage in practices that have a long history of producing no more than failure and frustration. Now, I'm not sure all of this adds up to knowing *what it is like to be* autistic or neurotic. And I'm surely not a Freudian psychoanalyst, but I'm rather more confident that it does add up to this: not knowing what it is like to be our better self.

I've only been able to sample a few of the clinical conditions that display certain aspects of conscious life and awareness otherwise obscured by normal life. There are many other conditions, some of them quite harrowing, which would make the same point even more starkly. There is a wide range of psychiatric illnesses classified as *dissociative disorders,* which might involve large gaps in memory, or the adoption of new and multiple personalities seemingly having nothing to do with the "real life" of the patient. Another version, referred to as *depersonalization disorder,* finds the patient seeing himself at a distance and reflecting on his own behavior as if he were a different and disinterested witness. Within the framework of consciousness and awareness, these conditions are especially intriguing, for the patients have consciousness and are aware—often acutely aware.

We've come up with labels for these various conditions. We seem to be better at creating labels than treatments. Many of the treatments, even the successful ones, seem to work for reasons that cannot yet be fathomed.

Then too, there are the many altered states of consciousness. Some of these come about through meditation; some come about through the use and the misuse of drugs, and herbs, and alcohol. There's a vast and popular literature on all this, readily available—nearly unavoidable. I'll say nothing about it. I note only that, given the importance, the very centrality of healthy, self-controlled conscious resources, well, it's always wise to leave well enough alone.

Lecture Twelve
Consciousness and the End of Mental Life

Scope:

In this lecture, we consider the case of comatose patients in relation to the nature of consciousness, self-consciousness, and *epistemic justification*. Such issues raise the vexing question of criteria used to analyze mental states and the equally critical questions of ethics, rights, and duties in relation to those incapable of protecting their own rights. We end this course with the consideration that it is conscious life that defines our humanity.

Outline

I. The conventional doctrine of neurology and neuroanatomy claims that neurons in the central nervous system are not regenerative, but that doctrine is being challenged by recent research in genetics and developmental neurobiology, as well as by cases of coma patients who have recovered.

   A. Many such patients actually resume a life not unlike the one they had left behind before the trauma, but these cases are the exception to the rule.

   B. When the cells in the traumatized area of the brain die, deficits ensue, some of which can be overcome by rehabilitation, and some of which cannot.

      1. The degree of recovery tends to be greater in early childhood.

      2. The more extensive the involvement of the cerebral cortext, the greater the effects on consciousness and the various powers that depend on it: focused attention, problem-solving, general awareness, and cognitive modes of represenation.

      3. These powers may be severely degraded—even go undetected by the most careful means—in a patient who is otherwise seemingly "awake" and physiologically competent.

      4. Life-sustaining processes can continue to support the body's biological requirements even when cortical functions have all but ceased.

5. Even with all the data that modern machines can generate, confusion and doubt will prevail regarding a coma patient's mental state, as in the famous case of Terri Schiavo.
6. In one systematic study, investigators found that 17 of 40 persistent vegetative state (PVS) patients were misdiagnosed, and one-third displayed recovery during the period of the research.

II. Cases of comatose patients relate to matters growing out of the central issues raised in our earlier lectures. Consider the doctors' dilemma of deciding whether or not such a patient has some inner mental life.

A. Thomas Nagel's question— "What is like to be a bat?"—hearkens back to an argument developed by Aristotle in the 4th century B.C.

B. For Aristotle, the dividing line between plant and animal life was established by sensation.

C. Pulling together Nagel's and Aristotle's understandings, we might say that mental states, at least minimally, are states in which something is sensed.
   1. A generalization of this criterion is the proposition that any creature that is the subject of sensation is in a mental state.
   2. Moreover, any creature that is potentially the subject of sensation is potentially the possessor of a mental state, from which we can infer that to be the potential subject of sensation is to be *potentially* conscious and to be the actual subject of sensation is to *be* conscious.

D. Does putting Nagel and Aristotle together in this way make for a sound proposition?
   1. Any number of sensations are present as we dream, but wouldn't it be contradictory to state that a dreamer is conscious?
   2. There seem to be important differences between states of consciousness and states of self-consciousness.
   3. What distinguishes dream states from waking states is not consciousness per se but what in metaphysics is sometimes referred to as *epistemic justification*.

4. What we believe about happenings as we dream is without the quality and character of justification enjoyed by things experienced in the waking state; in the waking state, we can justify our reported experiences by sharing them—intersubjective agreement is possible.

5. This issue is relevant to issues involving comatose patients, at least those who, on recovery, claim to have overheard people talking while they were seemingly unconscious.

III. Let us rehearse the conventional wisdom that our discussion of coma patients raises on key questions in ethics and moral thought.

A. Beginning with our understanding of obligations and duties, we have the duty not to exploit or unjustly benefit from the vulnerabilities of others.

B. When we consider our duty relating to the rights of those who are incapable of protecting their own rights, we must confront the nature and limits of the duties of the caretaker.

C. These rights and duties do not apply to those who are "brain dead," though the criteria for "brain death" are controversial.

D. Another pertinent question is: Just how much by way of biological function must a creature have to enjoy some measure of respect?

E. While advances in medicine and personal health have resulted in a more active and flourishing older population, decline in old age—including intellectual decline caused by such conditions as Alzheimer's disease—attacks what we take to be the very essence of our humanity: our mental life.

F. People make living wills to guard against the preservation of their lives should they succumb to a mentally debilitating disease. On what criteria do they base their judgment of a life not worth living?

1. How do caretakers decide when to honor a living will or take lethal action?

2. The "slippery slope" argument proposes that we hold back lethal action in the clearest of cases, lest we take lethal action in less clear cases.

3. In the case of animals, it is only in the philosophy seminar that serious doubts are raised as to whether animals have consciousness.
4. We take it to be a measure of civilization that those least able to care for themselves are the beneficiaries of the solicitude of others.
5. We care not only about creatures that are subject to pain and suffering but about our own character.

G. Our humanity seems to begin and end with conscious life. It is how we use all the rest that serves as a final judgment on whether that consciousness was a gift or a test that we have failed.

Essential Reading:

Jennett, B., *The Vegetative State: Medical Facts, Ethical and Legal Dilemmas.*

Sacks, O., *The Man Who Mistook His Wife for a Hat.*

Supplementary Reading:

Andrews, K., L. Murphy, R. Munday, and C. Littlewood, "Misdiagnosis of the Vegetative State: Retrospective Study in a Rehabilitation Unit," *British Medical Journal* 313 (1996): 13–16.

Horner, P. J., and J. H. Gage, "Regenerating the Damaged Central Nervous System," *Nature* 401 (2000): 1.

Questions to Consider:

1. It is said that the law has a compelling interest in the protection of life. Does this interest extend to a determination of when and whether one might end one's own life?

2. To say that my life is "mine" is to say something different from saying that it is a possession. How is the difference to be understood?

Lecture Twelve—Transcript
Consciousness and the End of Mental Life

I shall begin this final lecture on consciousness with the story reported in the *Los Angeles Times*, July 4, 2006. It's an account of the remarkable recovery of a Mr. Terry Wallis, who awoke from a comatose state 19 years after falling unconscious. Although rare, recovery after prolonged periods in coma has been reported in the medical literature often enough. What is especially unusual in the case of Mr. Wallis, however, is what was found on examining anatomical changes in his brain. Thanks to technical advances that have given us scans and comparably sensitive techniques for examining the microanatomy of the nervous system, it's possible to detect even the slightest changes; this was the case in examining Mr. Wallace's brain after his recovery.

Now, I should say that if one were to consult the older textbooks in neurology and neuroanatomy, one would be instructed that neurons in the central nervous system are non-regenerative. Once lost, they're gone forever. Although that doctrine was subject to challenge even some years ago, based on recent research in genetics and developmental neurobiology, the general message is still affirmed as recently as 2000 in the prestigious journal, *Nature,* where we find investigators acknowledging that:

> It is self-evident that the adult mammalian brain and spinal cord do not regenerate after injury, but recent discoveries have forced a reconsideration of this accepted principle. … Notwithstanding [recent] advances, clear and indisputable evidence for adult functional regeneration remains to be shown.

So I say that's a fairly recent literature still indicating how little there is, if any, by way of regeneration. Well, Mr. Wallis certainly proves to be the exception to this general rule. It was found that in the areas of his brain largely unaffected by the initial trauma, there was indeed new neuronal growth—axons growing out to make new connections to various regions of the brain.

The same article included comments by Dr. Steven Laureys, a specialist from Belgium. A case such as Mr. Wallis's, he noted, can only require a reconsideration of how comatose patients—patients in allegedly "persistent vegetative states"—are to be cared for. As he said, "It obliges us to reconsider old dogmas."

And by the way, even more recent evidence shows that in patients judged to be in a persistent vegetative state, they can have MRI activity based on things they are told to think about even as they lay there motionless, activity showed by the MRI to be very much like what is shown when conscious, healthy people are given the same mindset.

Well, as I say, the medical literature is scarcely silent on recoveries of the sort shown by Mr. Wallace. I might mention just a few vignettes to convey what neurologists—at least the good ones—are prepared to accept as possibilities. There is actually a Coma Recovery Association, chaired by Dr. Mihai Dimancescu, which maintains records and offers advice in this very area. What is clear is that comatose patients can recover, even after months and years in totally non-communicative states. No two cases are alike, so very nearly any generalization is going to be a risky one. One case, involving a young woman in her third month of coma, then recovered, only to complain about a doctor who, each time he passed by her bed, would inform medical residents and interns that she would never wake up! She resented hearing that, though in coma. There are these cases in which comatose patients, on recovering, make clear that they heard most of what was said by those near their beds.

Some might recall the case of Brian Cressler, the victim of an auto accident, who was comatose for a year and a half. With good care and with loving and hopeful parents, young Brian began to recover after he was brought home; the process very slow, gradual, but progressive. In time, though confined to a wheelchair, he finally reentered an active life. The neurosurgeon who had operated on him was quoted as saying that, "When his parents come in with pictures of him hitting tennis balls in his wheelchair and swimming laps in a pool, well, it's hard to imagine."

In yet another case, that of Patricia Bull, a woman from New Mexico, recovery didn't begin for 16 years! Mrs. Bull had become anoxic while giving birth. Her oxygen-starved brain led to an enduring coma. Doctors had made clear to the family that she would never recover. Alas, on Christmas Eve—out of the blue—she informed her nurses verbally that she did not want her bedding disturbed!

Well, a lecture far longer than 30 minutes would be required even to begin to sample the large and various assortment of cases in which profoundly and persistently comatose patients begin to recover from a perpetual dream state declared to be their final state before death itself.

Many such patients actually resume a life not unlike the one they had left behind before the trauma. The argument here, of course, the subtle argument is, of all the specialties of medicine we don't want to develop, that of oracular medicine would be very high on the list.

But make no mistake. These are not the expected outcomes; and as of now, they are very much exceptions to a general rule. But I do say "as of now," for predictions in any area like this are extremely hazardous. On the whole, I do regard oracular medicine as a specialty worthy of neglect. If we can be certain of anything, it's that there can be very little progress where there is very little hope. Still, the brain is not like skin and bones. When traumatized, or infected, or poisoned, the cells in the affected areas die, and deficits ensue. Some of these can be overcome by rehabilitation; some, as of now, cannot.

The degree of recovery, all things being equal, tends to be far greater in early childhood before the overall system has become settled in its ways. Again now, all other things being equal—almost never the case—the degree of functional loss in those capacities we regard as *mental* is greatest when it's the cerebral cortex that is attacked. The more extensive the cortical involvement, generally the greater the effects on consciousness and the various powers that depend on consciousness: focused attention, problem solving, general awareness, cognitive modes of representation.

These powers may be severely degraded, even undetected by the most careful means, in a patient who is otherwise seemingly awake and physiologically competent. Such life-sustaining processes as respiration and cardiac function depend on structures below the level of the cerebral cortex, and these can continue to support the biological requirements of the body even when cortical functions have all but ceased.

One of the famous cases in this area is that of Karen Ann Quinlan, back in the 1970s, who displayed yet another variation on this theme. In her case, there were no signs of wakefulness, no tracking movements by the eyes, no evidence of any degree of conscious awareness, despite the fact that electrical signals from her brain—her electroencephalographic data—were nearly within normal limits.

At the end of the day, each case must be weighed and understood in its own terms by specialists with extensive experience and, yes, the "open mind," which is precisely what experience is supposed to cultivate. When all this is in place, and when all the machines have generated as much data as seem to be relevant to the given case, it is unfortunately inevitable that confusion and doubt may still prevail.

These cases I mention surely will have many today thinking of Terri Schiavo. She, too, had spent years of her life in what was called a persistent vegetative state—the now well-known PVS, made part of the world's working vocabulary as the Schiavo tragedy worked its way through the courts. I should insert here another caution, this one pertaining to PVS. Keep in mind that the desire for economy of effort often leads us to reduce to a simple code or acronym what is in fact extremely complex and even utterly unsettled. PVS does not have the status of DNA, or of MC^2 or, for that matter, even of CNN.

After the death of Terri Schiavo, achieved by starving and dehydrating her, an autopsy was performed. Dr. Stephen Nelson, reporting to the chief medical examiner for the 10th Judicial Circuit of Florida offered these instructive lines on page 20 of his report: "Neuropathological examination alone of the decedent's brain—or any brain, for that matter, cannot prove or disprove a diagnosis of persistent vegetative state or minimally conscious state."

Actually, the diagnosis is not that straightforward. In fact, in one systematic study, investigators found that 17 of 40 so-called PVS patients were misdiagnosed, and fully one-third of them displayed recovery during the very period of the research. As the investigators in that study noted, "The vegetative state needs considerable skill to diagnose, requiring assessment over a period of time; diagnosis cannot be made, even by the most experienced clinician, from a bedside assessment."

Let me stay with Schiavo. For many years, Terri Schiavo was provided with no rehabilitative regimen as a battle in the courts was waged between her parents and her husband. The latter claimed to be doing his wife's bidding by allowing her to die. Her parents were of a different mind, and hoped that, under their care, she might recover some measure of mental life. Indeed, they were fairly confident that she already possessed some measure of mental life, though seriously limited in the extent to which she could express it.

The details of this case, as with the details of other cases I've mentioned, go far beyond the limits of a 30-minute lecture. What such cases do pick up, however, are matters growing out of the central issues raised in the previous lectures. Recall the issues surrounding the question of *other minds*.

Consider in that light the dilemma faced by a doctor who must advise a family as to whether or not a loved one still possesses some inner mental life. Consider also the relative cost of assuming that there is such a life, when in fact there isn't; as opposed to assuming that there is no such life, when in fact, there is. Well, when in doubt, toward which of these possibilities should we be inclined?

Recall, also, Thomas Nagel's, "What is it like to be a bat?" The question itself hearkens to an argument that Aristotle developed in the 4th century B.C. Aristotle would use the phrase, *to ti ein einai* ("what it is to be a given sort of thing," in Greek), which matches up closely enough with the notion of being a certain kind of entity. Now, for Aristotle, the dividing line between plant and animal life, as I've said, is established by sensation. To be able to sense, to be the subject of experience: on this account, that capacity virtually defines the class of beings we call *animal;* the class within which we include ourselves. Although I would not impute to Aristotle a recognition of the sense in which consciousness is understood to be problematical in contemporary philosophy, he certainly had the concept of consciousness. He does, after all, speak of our perceiving *that we are perceiving.*

Well, pulling together Aristotle's and Nagel's understandings, we might say that mental states, at least minimally, are states in which something is sensed, if only in the most minimal way. Thus, what it is like to be in a mental state, is to be in a state in which something is being sensed.

Now, we can proceed from this criterion, and offer as a plausible generalization from it, the proposition that any creature that is the subject of sensation is in a mental state. Moreover, any creature that is potentially the subject of sensation is potentially the possessor of a mental state. Let me put it most economically: the inference would then be that to be the potential subject of sensation is to be potentially conscious; and to be the actual subject of sensation is to be conscious.

Is this is a sound proposition? After all, any number of sensations—sights, sounds, for example—are present as we dream. Would it not be contradictory to state that a dreamer is conscious? Moreover, there are periods of daydreaming and idle reflection, when we seem not to be aware of any specific sensations at all, although we're certainly conscious.

Well, I have no ambition to create a new way of speaking or to challenge conventional meanings. It does seem to me, however, that there are important differences between states of consciousness and states of self-consciousness. To the extent that someone in a dream state is hearing sound and seeing sights, I don't know any other way of expressing things than to say that they are conscious of sights and sounds. Indeed, if at this very time they recognize themselves to be the subject of these experiences, then I don't know any other way of expressing things than to say that they are self-consciously aware, though dreaming.

I would be prepared to argue that what sets dream states off from waking states is not consciousness per se, but what in metaphysics is sometimes referred to as (here's a 24-carat term) *epistemic justification*. What we take to be the case in a dream state—what we believe about the happenings as we dream—is without a quality and character of justification enjoyed by things experienced in the waking state; for in the waking state, we can justify our reported experiences—how?—well, by sharing them. Thus, there is an apple on the table, and if you don't believe me, why don't you look? In the waking state, there is at least the possibility of intersubjective agreement, and this is precisely what's lacking in the dream state.

Mind you, I fully respect the difference between the two states. I'm no skeptic regarding wakefulness. Therefore, I respect the different senses of being conscious. There is awareness in dream states. There is, then, consciousness in dream states, as far as I've been able to develop the point. But it is not *waking* consciousness. It's not the consciousness that participates so essentially in interpersonal life. It's a consciousness stripped of all social uses.

Why do I tarry on this point? Because I regard it as relevant to issues involving comatose patients; at least the ones who, on recovery, claim to have heard much during the period of seeming unconsciousness. And I regard the issues involving comatose patients as relevant to fundamental questions in ethics and in moral thought.

I mustn't bite off too much here. I will not attempt to answer the fundamental questions. Nor will I suggest that these weighty issues admit of simple solutions, or even unarguable ones. Instead, I would hope to rehearse the conventional wisdom on a number of key points, and assess just how wise this wisdom is.

Perhaps the best starting point here is our understanding of obligations or duties. On what basis are we said to have a duty to others? Presumably, our duties in some complex way match up with, or come about as a result of, what we are prepared to regard as the rights of others. Indeed, it's commonplace, though somewhat erroneous, I think, to state that rights and duties entail each other. But there is a relationship between the two. Rights, of course, is a notoriously difficult concept. Jeremy Bentham notoriously referred to natural rights as "nonsense on stilts"!

This is yet another place, however, where a commonsense approach might be the wiser. Rights, as we are inclined to claim them, and as courts are inclined to honor them, arise from certain vulnerabilities that we have. All other things being equal, I have a right to be secure in my life and in my possessions. I have a right to be spared pain and suffering. Any number of subsidiary rights will arise from these basic ones. The basic ones have to do with the vulnerabilities that come about as a result of one's very biological and psychological constitution. Again, all other things being equal, we have the duty not to exploit, or enlarge, or unjustly benefit from, the vulnerabilities of others; their sense of being innocent and non-threatening others is the sense in which we are not to exploit their vulnerabilities.

Now, there are occasions in which the rights of others must be sacrificed by the others themselves. This seems to be characteristic of saints and heroes. And there are still other occasions in which rights are lost by others, owing to their abuse of these very rights. However, except in the interest of public safety, or as a means of self-defense, we have a duty to respect the rights of others and to understand that this duty is firm and fixed.

Well, we might now might consider the general question, just how much by way of biological or psychological function must a creature have to enjoy some measure of respect? And tied to this question is another: What is our duty in relation to the rights of others where those others are incapable of protecting their own rights? This question forces us to confront the nature and limits of the duties of the caretaker. Included in the category of caretaker are, of course, parents; teachers; the police; doctors and nurses; friends and neighbors; even total strangers, when another is defenseless and in need.

At least as I have summarized rights and duties here, I should think there would be total agreement with the proposition that we do not have duties to the dead, as such; though there are grounds on which we should be respectful. I mention this to say that, excluded from my remarks are those who qualify as being *brain dead* and, therefore, are dead. The criteria of brain death are themselves somewhat controversial. Summarizing the law in Massachusetts, the Massachusetts General Hospital puts it this way: "Death by brain criteria is defined under Massachusetts state law as the total and irreversible cessation of spontaneous brain functions, in which further attempts of resuscitation or continued supportive maintenance would not be successful in restoring such function."

Well, the cases I've discussed earlier in this lecture simply don't qualify. None of the patients, including Terry Schiavo, was brain dead. Of such patients, therefore, the two questions remain lively and insistent: Just how much, by way of biological or psychological function, must a creature have to enjoy some measure of respect? What is our duty in relation to the rights of others, where those others are incapable of protecting their own rights?

It's obvious that the higher we set the bar, the more likely it is we're going to fail in our duty to those who fully warrant concern and respect. It is worth pondering this fact. As of the first decade of the new millennium, there is only one state in the United States the majority of whose population is over 65 years of age. But by the year 2050, this will be true of 44 states. Advances in medicine, in sound personal health habits—well, these are likely to continue to make the later years far more active and flourishing than has been the case in earlier times.

Still, decline is a general rule, not a general exception, and mental decline is included in the total package. In this, needless to say, there are wide variations in the general population. It is not unusual for persons in their 80s and 90s to have rich and resourceful mental powers, and to remain intellectually alive as long as life persists. But, sad to say, it is also not unusual late in life for the net effects of small cerebral accidents and for still other assaults on one's general physiology to become manifest in the form of intellectual decline.

The limiting case is that of Alzheimer's disease. Here, in the advanced states of life, life is lived in a perpetual twilight; the most familiar sights now unrecognized; the relationships of a lifetime lost to memory, and no longer eliciting the desires and feelings so dependent on memory.

Comparably disabling and limiting are the most severe forms of mental retardation, calling for constant vigilance on the part of caregivers, and creating a life of nearly total dependency.

Now, these are examples of conditions that attack what we take to be our most defining attribute; what we take to be the very essence of our humanity, which is to say, our mental life.

This much said, not only do the ethical questions not go away, they return with a vengeance. How many times are we asked to understand such difficult cases in terms of questions of the sort, "Is this the sort of life *you* would want to live?" as if the answer to that question could settle anything. What of instances in which the patient herself, earlier in life and competent, declared that she wouldn't want to be maintained in such a state of existence? What of instances where someone has actually composed a living will? Here the desires and intentions are set down in black letters: If I am ever in a state of such and such a nature, it is my desire that no further means be employed to preserve my life, etc. The problem, of course, is tied to the phrase, "of such and such a nature."

We do not know what it is like to be a bat; we do not know what it is like to be in coma. We can't even say that we know what it's like to be sleeping. We can say what it is like to be restored to consciousness after sleeping. If there are no dreams during our sleep, then the sleeping life is an empty life. We might say of such a life that it's not like being anything. We protect that life on the assumption that, come the morning, its normal functions will be restored. Suppose it was the case, however, that such functions were only restored every two days; every eight days; twice a year, but only briefly. I assume the point is clear. Actions that end life are irretrievable. If we are mistaken at that point, there is no going back.

Commentators on issues of this sort frequently invoke the metaphor of the slippery slope. According to this way of saying the problem, we hold back lethal action in the clearest of cases, lest we take lethal action in less clear cases.

The same commentators, however, tend to give dispositive power to the potential victim. "Whose life is it anyway?" is thought to be a question that answers itself. But does it? We do not live in isolation from all other beings. What we say through our laws defines us. When we use the instrument of law in order to establish within our species the types that we regard as less than human, we give a certain definition to our own humanity.

It is only in the philosophy of the seminar room that serious doubts are raised as to whether or not dogs, and cats, and other animals have consciousness. We all know how aware they are of their surroundings, and of us. They leave no doubt when they are in pain. And, recognizing this, civilized people set limits on the degree to which such creatures can be used or abused. And we take it to be a measure of civilization, that those least able to care for themselves are the beneficiaries of the solicitude of others. We would not permit the record of our own humanity to be sullied by a willingness to inflict pain, and suffering, and death on those who, for some inexplicable reason, asked us to do it! We not only care about creatures subject to pain and suffering, we care about our own character. And that character expresses itself, and develops itself; it refines itself, in just those settings in which even the wishes of others cannot defeat the principle that we take to be the very grounding of our humanity.

Our humanity. It seems to begin and end with conscious life, with consciousness. It's this that opens the door to all the rest. And it's how we use all the rest that serves final judgment on whether that consciousness was a gift, or a test that we have failed.

Glossary

Aharanov-Bohm effect: Refers to effects produced by an electromagnetic field in regions otherwise fully shielded.

algorithm: A "recipe" of sorts for accomplishing specific tasks or solving specific problems.

Alzheimer's disease: An age-related disease whose most devastating symptom is dementia. It affects about five percent of those between 65 and 75 but as many as half of those over 85.

anomalous monism: Donald Davidson's term referring to the inability to translate mental terms directly into physical terms, even while accepting that all mental states refer to what at base are physical states.

antirealism: A thesis in philosophy of science that rejects the view of scientific laws as veritable pictures or exact reflections of reality.

artificial intelligence: The seemingly intelligent behavior of computational systems powerful enough to solve complex problems.

artificial language: Thomas Reid's term for any developed language of words and grammar.

Asperger's syndrome: One of the autism-related disorders, milder than autism proper.

attention deficit hyperactivity disorders (ADHD): Term covering a range of symptoms that include impulsive behavior and inability to maintain focused attention.

auditory defensiveness: A symptom of autism such that the patient becomes defensively unresponsive to disturbing sounds.

autism: A pervasive developmental disorder involving language, behavior, and social interactions, the symptoms appearing early in childhood and often associated with a degree of mental retardation.

autism spectrum disorders: A group of disorders that includes autism and Asperger's disease.

autoscopy: The seeming ability to see oneself from a position external to one's actual location; e.g., "out-of-body" experiences.

brain death: A condition of the brain satisfying widely adopted criteria within neurology and including absence of recordable electrical activity.

"Chinese nation" analogy: Ned Block's fanciful analogy to the nervous system, here, with each citizen of China equipped to function as a neuron. Each citizen is able to enter a complex network of information via phone calls that mimic perfectly the signals generated in an individual's nervous system and are associated with the sensation of pain, although no one in China thus experiences pain.

"Chinese room": John Searle's famous room analogy in which persons ignorant of Chinese nonetheless arrange Chinese ideograms according to rules. The result is a message meaningful to those who know the Chinese language but not to those who assemble the message.

cocktail party effect: The ability to maintain focused attention on one's own conversations in a setting in which loud noise is "filtered" out.

compulsion: A neurotic repetition of stereotypic behaviors.

Deep Blue: The IBM computer that defeated Garry Kasparov.

demonstrative: A mode of argument leading to conclusions seen to be both certain and logically necessary.

depersonalization disorder: A form of mental illness in which one feels detached from one's own body and experiences.

dichotic: A mode of presentation of sounds in which each ear receives a separate input.

dissociative disorder: Exemplified by "multiple personality" and often related to traumatic experiences in early childhood.

dualism: The thesis that there are two basic and different constituents of reality, one physical and one mental.

efficient cause: Typically, the event immediately preceding an effect and having a measurable, physical influence, such as one billiard ball hitting another.

empirical: Accessible to direct or aided observation.

Enlightenment: The 18th-century epoch of heightened intellectual and revolutionary undertakings, impelled by unstinting confidence in science.

entropy: The tendency toward disorder. In thermodynamics, the byproduct of work in the form of heat; in cosmology, the forces that oppose order and coherence.

epistemology: The branch of metaphysics devoted to a critical appraisal of knowledge claims and the modes of inquiry and explanation on which such claims are based.

Essentialism: The thesis that specific "kinds" of things (apples, persons, copper) are what they are owing to certain core and defining properties.

explanatory gap: The "gap" in an otherwise completely physical account of reality; the gap arising from the resistance of mental phenomena to physicalistic explanations.

final cause: In Aristotle's sense, the "that for the sake of which" other causal modalities are recruited; the goal or end toward which actions tend.

formal cause: In Aristotle's sense, the feature that makes a thing the sort of thing it is; the difference between a collection of bricks and a house is that the latter has the requisite form of a house.

Functionalism: The thesis that the right understanding and explanation of any process is in terms of the functions it serves; two systems are relevantly the same when they perform the same functions.

Gödel's theorem: The proof that any mathematical system of sufficient power to include arithmetic depends on axioms that cannot be proved within the system itself. All such systems are, in this sense, "incomplete."

identity of indiscernibles: A version of Leibniz's law of identity; X and Y are identical to the extent that they cannot be discerned separately.

identity thesis: An attempted solution to the mind-body problem based on the thesis that events in the brain do not cause mental events, but that the latter are simply the brain events themselves.

imitation game: Alan Turing's term for the game used to show that a concealed machine, properly programmed to answer questions, will be indistinguishable from an intelligent human being.

incorrigibility: Not subject to correction; our statements about our own pains and perceptions are said to be "incorrigible" in this sense.

intentionality: A term indebted to Franz Brentano and capturing the "aboutness" of mental events. Thoughts, beliefs, and desires are "about" their objects in a way that distinguishes such mental events in principle from anything that is merely physical.

intuitive: A mode of knowing that results in immediate and certain knowledge; for example, that up is not down, black is not white, and so on.

Laplace's demon: That super mind postulated (as impossible) by Laplace that, equipped with knowledge of the position and momentum of every particle of physical reality and the laws of physics, would unerringly predict all future events.

law of contradiction: It is not possible for something to be and simultaneously not be.

Leibniz's law: See **identity of indiscernibles**.

"Mary" problem: A thought experiment devised by Frank Jackson in an attempt to show that qualia exist and to refute the physicalist solution to the mind-body problem.

material cause: In Aristotle's sense, the matter that is necessary for something to be the subject of other causal influences.

mental causation: Thoughts, desires, and motives bringing about musculo-skeletal events.

metaphysics: The branch of philosophy addressed to the question of *being* as such; the ultimate contents of reality.

Monistic idealism: The thesis that the ultimate reality is not physical but mental and that the physical world, to the extent that it exists at all, does so in a totally mind-dependent fashion.

Monistic materialism: The contents of reality include only material kinds of "stuff."

natural language: In Thomas Reid's philosophy especially, the classification of innate tendencies toward facial expressions, posture, vocalization, and so forth as "natural" means of communication.

nominal essence: John Locke's term for the properties of reality that we assign to things in the form of names; a reality reflecting not the core physicality of things but our conventional ways of knowing them. See **real essence**.

obsession: A neurotic state of mind in which an idea or theme cannot be abandoned.

Ontology: The philosophical specialty devoted to the question "What is there?"

other minds: An issue in philosophy arising from the fact that we have direct access only to our own thoughts, desires, and beliefs and, therefore, that our assumption that there is any mind other than our own is groundless.

persistent vegetative state (PVS): A term in clinical neurology referring to patients in an enduring comatose state, with ostensible signs of mental life but with these being purely reflexive.

personal identity: The conventional term in philosophy referring to the continuity of one's "self" over time and amidst all the biological and social changes to which one is subject.

philosophy of mind: The branch of philosophy devoted to an examination of the "mental" and its relation to the balance of reality.

Physicalism: A thesis committed to the position that all reality is, at base, physical.

Pragmatism: A standard less of "truth" than of the grounds on which claimed truth finds its ultimate test.

Qualia: The subjective properties of things as experienced, for example, tastes, colors, sounds.

Quantum physics: The physics of the ultimately small and the forces governing their behavior.

real essence: Locke's term for what is the ultimate reality of a thing; its invisible but physical substrate having nothing in common with that "nominal essence" assigned to it by convention.

Realism: In philosophy of science, the thesis that the laws of science are accurate and direct depictions of reality as such.

rigid designator: Saul Kripke's term for an ontological status that obtains "in all possible worlds." *Pain* is a rigid designator in that, wherever it is and under any set of descriptions or contexts, pain is pain.

romantic rebellion: A term referring to the aesthetic reaction against the claims and methods of science.

solipsism: The thesis that all reality, known as it is solely through one's own mental representations, exists only in these representations.

somnambulism: Sleep-walking.

Spandrel: In architecture, a feature not intended to function in the way it does but brought about by the arrangement of other structures having a definite function. Within evolutionary theory, the metaphor of the spandrel is intended to convey the appearance of something not itself "selected" but arising from features that were.

substance: In Aristotle's phrase, "that which is peculiar to it, which does not belong to anything else ... substance means that which is not predicable of a subject."

supervenience: A term covering the sequential dependencies from the most basic to the most apparent; thus, tables supervene on wood; wood supervenes on molecules; molecules on atoms, and so forth. On this account, the mental allegedly supervenes on the physical.

zombies: In philosophy of mind, a term for the "undead"; philosophical zombies are resourceful, though lacking all consciousness and self-awareness.

Biographical Notes

Aristotle (384–322 B.C.): Ancient Greek philosopher and scientist whose concepts form the basis for much of the Western intellectual tradition.

George Berkeley (1685–1753): A master of optics and mathematics and defender of a form of *idealism* designed to defeat the skeptical implications of materialism. Late in life, he would be appointed bishop of Cloyne.

Ned Block (1942–): Harvard trained, former Chair of Philosophy at the Massachusetts Institute of Technology (MIT), and now Professor of Philosophy at New York University (NYU). Opposed the Turing-test approach to establishing the nature of intelligent behavior; an important contributor to issues involving computational models of human cognition.

David Bohm (1917–1992): A contributor to the Manhattan Project, an associate of Albert Einstein, and a major figure in the development of quantum physics. The charged political climate of the 1950s resulted in his self-exile from the United States.

Franz Brentano (1838–1917): Devoted his early scholarship to the philosophy of Aristotle and was later ordained as a Roman Catholic priest. He abandoned the priesthood over the issue of papal infallibility. His *Psychology from an Empirical Standpoint* (1874) developed the concept of "intentionality" as it would figure in philosophy of mind.

Paul Churchland (1942–): Professor of Philosophy at the University of California, San Diego, Churchland is the quintessential physicalist in the matter of mind and mental life, ardently advocating nothing less than a "neurophilosophy."

Donald Davidson (1917–2003): Among the most influential figures in contemporary philosophy, known especially for his analysis of causal explanation and the putative distinction between "reasons" and "causes" as accounts of significant human actions. His academic life was spent at Stanford (1951–1967), Princeton (1967–1970), the Rockefeller University (1970–1976), the University of Chicago (1976–1981), and from 1981 until his death, Berkeley.

Daniel Dennett (1942–): University Professor and Austin B. Fletcher Professor of Philosophy and Director of the Center for Cognitive Studies at Tufts University. Dennett is one of the half-dozen most influential writers and theorists in the field of cognitive neuroscience.

Kurt Gödel (1906–1978): Czech-born and one of the leading logicians of the modern age, publishing his incompleteness theorem at the age of 25. For many years, a Fellow of Princeton's Institute for Advanced Study.

Thomas Hobbes (1588–1679): Educated in classics at Oxford; a royalist during the Cromwell years and, thus, exiled in Holland. Impressed by the works and research of Galileo, Hobbes developed political and moral theories based on physical-mechanistic principles, and he examined the nature of political organization within a mechanistic framework.

David Hume (1711–1776): Arguably, the most influential philosopher in the English language. He did much to absorb traditional problems in epistemology and ethics into an essentially psychological framework, arguing against the objectivity of morals and the proposition that "truth" is ever independent of the mental processes devoted to its discovery.

Edmund Husserl (1859–1938): German philosopher, student of Brentano, and recognized father of phenomenology. His treatise on ideas (*Ideen*) in 1913 drew attention to the difference between the act of consciousness and the phenomena toward which it is directed.

Frank Jackson (1943–): Currently Distinguished Professor at the Australian National University, where he has also served as Professor of Philosophy and head of the Philosophy Program, as well as Director of the University's Institute of Advanced Studies.

William James (1842–1910): American philosopher and psychologist who led the movements in pragmaticism and functionalism. His functionalistic approach to the mind-body problem is seen by some as the culmination of late-19th-century thought on the subject.

Garry Kasparov (1963–): Russian-born grandmaster and, at the time of the match with Deep Blue, widely regarded as perhaps the greatest chess player of all time.

Saul Kripke (1940–): Influential philosopher of language; Professor of Philosophy at Princeton and at the City University of New York; offers formidable arguments against mind-brain identity theories.

Pierre-Simon Laplace (1749–1827): Precocious in his mastery of mathematics, Laplace would find a tutor and supporter in d'Alembert in Paris, where, over a course of years, he contributed significantly to several branches of mathematics, especially differential equations and probability theory.

Gottfried Leibniz (1646–1716): German philosopher and logician, inventor (independently of Newton) of differential and integral calculus, and a significant contributor to the widest range of intellectual and philosophical issues.

John Locke (1632–1704): Oxford educated, a father of British empiricism, a major influence on the philosophical and political thought of the modern world, and a talented physician.

Thomas Nagel (1937–): Born in Belgrade, earned the B. Phil. from Oxford and Ph.D. from Harvard. Currently Professor of Philosophy and of Law at New York University.

Roger Penrose (1931–): Fellow of Balliol College, Oxford, knighted for his contributions to mathematics and science; brother of Jonathan Penrose, a chess grandmaster. His arguments against the possibility of today's physics to explain consciousness are profound, influential, and controversial.

Thomas Reid (1710–1796): Father of Scottish "Common Sense" philosophy; best known for his anti-skeptical arguments against David Hume and as a staunch defender of the methods of Bacon and Newton in approaching the nature of mind and mental life.

Oliver Sacks (1933–): London-born and Oxford-trained neurologist, Sacks has written with cogency and poignancy on the complexities of brain function as revealed in the neurology clinic.

Jean-Paul Sartre (1905–1980): Earned a doctorate in philosophy and became a leader of the existentialist school of philosophy. His essays and fiction did much to underscore the separation between an indifferent world external to consciousness and the lived life afforded by this recognition.

John Searle (1932–): U.S.-born Oxford Rhodes Scholar and Oxford-trained philosopher; Slusser Professor of Philosophy at Berkeley; a major figure in philosophy of mind and philosophy of language.

J. J. C. Smart (1920–): Scots-Australian, Oxford-educated philosopher and member of the philosophy faculty of the Australian National University; a significant figure in philosophy of mind, defending a form of mind-brain "identity."

Alan Turing (1912–1954): British mathematician, one of the fathers of today's computer science, and one of the great "code breakers" of World War II. His original contributions to mathematics were foundational for today's information sciences.

Johann Wolfgang von Goethe (1749–1832): Genius of Romantic intellectualism, his philosophical contributions laid the foundation for later developments in German idealism and phenomenology; acute commentator on scientific matters and early advocate of evolutionary principles.

Eugene Wigner (1902–1995): Winner of the 1963 Nobel Prize in Physics; born in Budapest, Hungary, he became a U.S. citizen in 1937 and was, for many years, Thomas D. Jones Professor of Mathematical Physics at Princeton University.

Ludwig Wittgenstein (1889–1951): A genius of the modern world, Austrian- born to one of the wealthiest of Viennese families. His years at Cambridge with Bertrand Russell found him challenging the received wisdom of traditional philosophy, his major tool of criticism being a special form of linguistic analysis.

Bibliography

Essential Reading:

Albert, D. *Quantum Mechanics and Experience*. Cambridge: Harvard University Press, 1992. To quote the book jacket: "Ever since physics first penetrated the atom, what it found there has stood as a radical and unanswered challenge to many of our most cherished conceptions of nature."

Armstrong, D. M. *A Materialist Theory of the Mind*. London: Routledge, 1968. This is a now "classic" defense of philosophical materialism and a criticism of alternative perspectives.

Avramides, A. *Other Minds*. London: Routledge, 2001. Perhaps the best recent work on the subject. The author carefully sets forth the problem of other minds, various attempts at a solution, and a cogent "commonsense" defense.

Block, N., O. Flanagan, and G. Güzeldere, eds. *The Nature of Consciousness: Philosophical Debates*. Cambridge: MIT Press, 1997. A number of the major issues covered in these lectures are addressed in the chapters of this book.

Bohm, D., and B. J. Hiley. *The Undivided Universe*. London: Routledge, 1993. The authors "undivide" the universe by attempting to account for consciousness and the "mental" in a manner compatible with quantum physics.

Chalmers, D. J. *The Conscious Mind: In Search of a Fundamental Theory*. New York: Oxford University Press, 1996. David Chalmers provides an extensive bibliography and thoughtful discussions of central issues in philosophy of mind. It is perhaps the best introduction to the subject.

Güzeldere, Güven "Three Ways of Being a Zombie." Presented at the University of Arizona conference, *Toward a Science of Consciousness*, April 8–13, 1996, Tucson, AZ. www.conferencerecording.com/conflists/tsc96.htm. The author reviews various types of zombie: behavioristic, functionalistic, and physical clone. The assets and liabilities of each model are discussed in relation to various philosophies of mind.

Heil, J., and A. Mele, eds. *Mental Causation*. Oxford: Clarendon Press, 1993. Chapters in this volume clearly examine and assess the difficulties encountered in attempts to explain mental-physical causal relationships.

Hurley, S. *Consciousness in Action*. Cambridge: Harvard University Press, 1998. This major work by Susan Hurley is quite technical in places but draws attention to a number of the subtler aspects of the problem of consciousness.

Jackson, F. "What Mary Didn't Know." *Journal of Philosophy* 83 (1986): 291–295. This is the article by Jackson that more or less put the ball in play.

James, W. "Does Consciousness Exist?" *Journal of Philosophy, Psychology, and Scientific Methods* 1 (1904): 477–491. (Easily obtained either on the Internet or in anthologies of William James's major works). James in this essay rejects "consciousness" as an entity and defends it as a function—the function of "knowing."

———. *Principles of Psychology* (1890). Cambridge: Harvard University Press, 1983. Perhaps the finest and surely the most well written introduction to the subject.

Jennett, B. *The Vegetative State: Medical Facts, Ethical and Legal Dilemmas*. New York: Cambridge University Press, 2002. A landmark exploration of the state of wakeful unconsciousness; the author is a noted neurosurgeon.

Kim, J., ed. *Supervenience and Mind: Selected Philosophical Essays*. Cambridge: Cambridge University Press, 1993. Kim has been the leading defender of supervenience theory as a solution to the mind-body problem. This volume includes his most influential work.

Levine, J. *Purple Haze: The Puzzle of Consciousness*. New York: Oxford University Press, 2001. Levine discusses the "explanatory gap," underscoring the peculiar nature of consciousness in an otherwise mindless world of physical objects.

Lockwood, M. *Mind, Brain, and the Quantum: The Compound 'I'*. New York: Oxford University Press, 1989. Michael Lockwood offers an original application of quantum physics to philosophy of mind. It is the best book on this subject.

McGinn, C. *The Mysterious Flame: Conscious Minds in a Material World*. New York: Basic Books, 1999. Entirely accessible to a general audience, this book regards consciousness as simply being beyond the reach of scientific or philosophical explanation. The book is all the more compelling because its author is an accomplished philosopher.

Nagel, T. "What Is It Like to Be a Bat?" *Philosophical Review* 4 (1974): 435–450. Reprinted in *Mortal Questions* (Cambridge

University Press, 1979). This proved to be one of the seminal articles on the core issue of consciousness. It is among the most cited articles in contemporary philosophy.

Penrose, R. *The Emperor's New Mind: Concerning Computers, Minds, and the Laws of Physics.* Oxford: Oxford University Press, 1989. Penrose here develops the strongest arguments against computational models of mental life.

Poland, J. *Physicalism: The Philosophical Foundations.* Oxford: Clarendon Press, 1994. A good, clear, and generous exposition of physicalism.

Robinson, D. N., ed. *The Mind (Oxford Readers).* New York: Oxford University Press, 1998. Dozens of original articles appear in this anthology, with extensive introductions to the major sections.

Sacks, O. *The Man Who Mistook His Wife for a Hat.* New York: Simon & Schuster, 1985. A handful of astonishing cases from the neurology clinic and a gentle reminder of the complexity of mental life as actually lived.

Searle, J. R. *The Rediscovery of the Mind.* Cambridge: MIT Press, 1992. In this work, John Searle challenges any number of computational approaches and presents his own neuropsychological position on mind and mental life.

Strawson, G. *Mental Reality.* Cambridge: MIT Press, 1994. This is a vigorous defense of a radically materialistic philosophy of mind.

Supplementary Reading:

Andrews, K., L. Murphy, R. Munday, and C. Littlewood. "Misdiagnosis of the Vegetative State: Retrospective Study in a Rehabilitation Unit." *British Medical Journal*, 313 (1996): 13–16. This research leads to the conclusion that, in the diagnosis of persistent vegetative states (PVS), errors are quite common, even on the part of otherwise well-trained and experienced physicians.

Armstrong, D. M., and N. Malcolm. *Consciousness and Causality: A Debate on the Nature of Mind.* Oxford: Blackwell, 1984. David Armstrong takes a committed materialist position on consciousness. Norman Malcolm, in the patrimony of Wittgenstein, offers constructive challenges.

Baron-Cohen, S. *Mindblindness: An Essay on Autism and Theory of Mind.* Cambridge: MIT Press, 1997. Here, the reader confronts the phenomena arising from autism and the bearing of such clinical conditions on our understanding of mental life.

Bealer, G. "Self-consciousness." *Philosophical Review* 106 (1997): 69–117. This is a closely argued account of the nature of self-consciousness and the problems it presents to philosophy of mind.

Carruthers, P. *Phenomenal Consciousness: A Naturalistic Theory.* New York: Cambridge University Press, 2000. The author attempts to absorb qualia into a larger naturalistic framework, rendering a scientific approach to the problem at least plausible.

Catalano, J. *Thinking Matter: Consciousness from Aristotle to Putnam and Sartre.* New York: Routledge, 2000. As the subtitle suggests, philosophers from ancient Greece to our own time have wrestled with the question of how a material entity comes to have conscious life.

Crick, F., and C. Koch. "Why Neuroscience May Be Able to Explain Consciousness." *Scientific American* 273 (6): 84–85 (1995). Francis Crick is a Nobel laureate. In this article, he and Koch offer what might be regarded as an especially optimistic view on the extent to which science will explain consciousness.

Dennett, D. C. "The Unimagined Preposterousness of Zombies." *Journal of Consciousness Studies* 2 (1995): 322–326. Whether or not there can be zombies is a serious question. Dennett lays down interesting skeptical arguments.

Flanagan, O. J. *Consciousness Reconsidered.* Cambridge: MIT Press, 1992. Flanagan leaves no doubt about his own position: Consciousness is real, plays an important causal role, and resides in the brain.

Foss, J. *Science and the Riddle of Consciousness: A Solution.* Amsterdam: Kluwer, 2000. Yet another attempt to demystify consciousness and render it accessible to scientific research and theory.

Güzeldere, G. "Varieties of Zombiehood." *Journal of Consciousness Studies* 2 (1995): 326–333. In this article, the various candidate zombies are described, and their place within philosophical discourse is nicely reviewed.

Harnad, S. "Why and How We Are Not Zombies." *Journal of Consciousness Studies* 1 (1994): 164–167. Another serious if not fully successful critique of the "zombie" issue within philosophy of mind.

Heisenberg, W. *Physics and Philosophy*. New York: Harper and Row, 1958. Here, one of the great scientists of the 20th century considers the philosophical problems faced by modern physics and the implications to be drawn from these problems.

Hobbes, T. *Leviathan* (1651). New York: Touchstone, 1997. One of the most important works of philosophy, this book was one of the earliest attempts to understand politics and society in their modern form. Hobbes's discussions on the nature of the individual are most pertinent to this course.

Horner, P. J., and J. H. Gage. "Regenerating the Damaged Central Nervous System." *Nature* 401 (2000). Recent evidence is offered here of the ability of central nervous system neurons to regenerate after injury.

Kim, J. "Mental Causation and Consciousness: The Two Mind-Body Problems for the Physicalist." In *Physicalism and Its Discontents*, edited by C. Gillett and B. Loewer. Cambridge: Cambridge University Press, 2001. An in-depth discussion of the "relationship between mind and matter," focused on mental causation and consciousness.

Kirk, R. *Raw Feeling: A Philosophical Account of the Essence of Consciousness*. New York: Oxford University Press, 1994. Kirk is interesting in that he is prepared to accept the mental but not as fundamental. He defines the physical as whatever physics finally includes as physical theory.

Locke, J. *An Essay Concerning Human Understanding*. Edited by P. Nidditch. Oxford: Clarendon Press, 1975. One of the classic works in philosophy of mind; a forceful defense of empirical theories of mind.

Lycan, W. G. *Consciousness and Experience*. Cambridge: MIT Press, 1996. A strong advocate of the "representational" theory of brain function, concluding that, "once representation itself is (eventually) understood, then not only consciousness in our present sense but subjectivity, qualia, 'what it's like,' and every other aspect of the mental will be explicable in terms of representation together with the underlying, functionally organized neurophysiology."

Nelkin, N. *Consciousness and the Origins of Thought*. Cambridge: Cambridge University Press, 1996. Defended here is the view of consciousness as an instance of "higher order" thought, consciousness as the system's reflections on its own operations.

O'Shaughnessy, B. *Consciousness and the World*. New York: Oxford University Press, 2000. The author says in his introduction, "Consciousness has from the start an appointment in the concrete, with the World in its ultimate physical form"; he then proceeds to integrate consciousness with perception and attention within the framework of adaptation.

Perry, J. *Knowledge, Possibility, and Consciousness*. Cambridge: MIT Press, 2001. A defender of physicalism, Perry advances a theory of "antecedent physicalism" and deploys it against various challenges to physicalism, including the zombie argument.

Robinson, H., ed. *Objections to Physicalism*. New York: Oxford University Press, 1993. Very good essays on the central postulates of physicalism and the challenge to them arising from mental life.

Sartre, J. *Being and Nothingness*. Translated by H. E. Barnes. New York: Philosophical Library, 1956. This is the "bible" of existentialism and a somewhat poetic precis on the limits of understanding.

Seager, W. E. *Theories of Consciousness: An Introduction and Assessment*. London: Routledge, 1999. This is a very useful introductory treatise. Some philosophical sophistication is required, but the presentations are sound and thoughtful.

Siewert, C. *The Significance of Consciousness*. Princeton: Princeton University Press, 1998. The author takes consciousness seriously. He challenges theories that equate consciousness with a functional role or with information processing. He does not underestimate the challenges posed by qualia and by the authority of first-person reports. He usefully includes clinical findings.

Turing, A. M. "Computing Machinery and Intelligence." *Mind* 49 (1950): 433–460. This is the "classic" defense of artificial intelligence by one of the true pioneers.

Tye, M. "Phenomenal Consciousness: The Explanatory Gap as a Cognitive Illusion." *Mind* 108 (1999): 705–725. Tye argues that there actually is no explanatory gap between consciousness and the physical once our conceptual house is put in order.

Notes